CONTENTS

SAID ABOUT IBSEN

– BY NORWEGIAN WRITERS

SAID ABOUT IBSEN

– BY NORWEGIAN WRITERS

Translated by Robert Ferguson

GYLDENDAL

Said About Ibsen – by Norwegian writers
is jointly produced by
Norwegian Ministry of Foreign Affairs
NORLA
and Gyldendal Norsk Forlag.

© Norwegian Ministry of Foreign Affairs
NORLA
and Gyldendal Norsk Forlag 2006
© Robert Ferguson 2006

**NORWEGIAN MINISTRY
OF FOREIGN AFFAIRS**

Printed in Denmark.
Printing/binding: Nørhaven Paperback
Typeface: Laboremus Prepress AS, Oslo
Paper: 60 g Ensolux cream (2,0)
Caricature of Henrik Ibsen: Olaf Gulbransson
© Olaf Gulbransson / BONO 2004
Cover design: Trond Fasting Egeland

ISBN 82-05-35611-4

IBSEN AS LIFE-RAFT

Foreword

A hundred years after his death Henrik Ibsen remains unquestionably Norway's most famous man internationally. According to the official website www.ibsen.net, he is the second most frequently performed dramatist in the world after Shakespeare. In the month of May 2005 alone we know of 125 performances, from Bangladesh to Brazil. He is the only Scandinavian writer to be included in Harold Bloom's canon (in his book *The Western Canon,* 1994), along with 13 other central writers: Shakespeare, Dante, Chaucer, Cervantes, Montaigne, Milton, Goethe, Wordsworth, Whitman, Tolstoy, Proust and Joyce.

How can a writer from a peripheral country like Norway attain a position of such prominence? Was he simply a rare talent who happened to be born among us, as Bloom provocatively suggests? ("His canonical position owes almost nothing to the social energies of the times")?

Even though no Norwegian writer of today can match up to Ibsen, our contemporary literature is nevertheless remarkably rich, bearing in mind that our population numbers just 4 million people. It is tempting to explain it by saying that, in fact, it is precisely the periphery that is central: Norway is a country of narrow valleys and tall mountains. It is the land of polar night, and so cold that one can ski over the frozen waters for half the year. One can either challenge the climate and the geography, or defer to it; for Norwegians this means that there are two ways of becoming world-famous: you can ski to the North Pole, as Roald Amundsen did, or stay indoors and invent stories, like Henrik Ibsen.

This partial, 'Norwegian' explanation for the Ibsen phenomenon is only half in jest. The heart of the matter is, of course, that Ibsen was first and foremost a European. And here I must disagree with Bloom and maintain that he could not have been who he was without Europe as his stage, and the social energies that were at work there: a time of great change, industrialization, the rise of a bourgeoisie, the spread of democracy – the whole rapid expansion of modernism.

Ibsen wrote his great plays during the 27 years spent living abroad, in Europe, and the plots of them unfold in small Norwegian towns and hidden-away fjord settlements. From his vantage point within large German cities, and already established as a name on the German stage, he turns the Norwegian town into an arena for the struggle between traditionalism and modernity. In doing so, his writing becomes universal. Of course he had talent, but he was also – supremely – in the right place at the right time. It is as though he can pick the entire tree clean of its ripe fruits because he arrives at the right time, just as Shakespeare did in what Bloom calls the age of the aristocrat.

Whether Ibsen was a genius, a product of history, or both, he was also dependent on an outstanding publisher. His search took him to Copenhagen, to Danish Gyldendal, with whom he published all his books from *Brand* in 1866 to *When We Dead Awaken* in 1899. The publisher was the celebrated Frederik Hegel, whom Ibsen's literary colleague Bjørnstjerne Bjørnson once, in a lyrical moment, called "the sweetest old provider known to any poet in the whole world". The more cautious Ibsen contented himself with the observation that "when you became my publisher it marked a turning point in my life, as it did in my fortune."

Gyldendal Norsk Forlag has been publishing Ibsen's writings since 1925, and in the centenary year of 2006 will be presenting a wide range of books by and about the dramatist. One of them is the series of 12 paperback books, with Afterwords written by living authors, which is the basis for this little book. The idea arose in discussions on how we might focus on Ibsen's relevance for modern Norwegian audiences and readers. There are those who claim that Norwegians fail to understand just how thrillingly relevant to contemporary life

Ibsen's writing actually is. But when we approached authors and intellectuals with our idea we received immediate confirmation of his standing in these circles. All of those we spoke to were enthused by the idea, and flattered at being invited to contribute. None asked for time to think the matter over.

The contributors were given the following brief: "Your Afterword should preferably not be aimed at an academic readership, nor should it necessarily involve a 'correct' understanding of the play. Our hope is that Ibsen will be read with fresh, new eyes." The result is the twelve Afterwords collected in this book on the initiative of the Foreign Department. They have been translated into English, French, Italian, Chinese, Russian, Spanish and German, and are part of the Ibsen programme abroad.

So we are commemorating the one hundredth anniversary of Ibsen's death. How highly is it reasonable for Norway to prize its great poet? Harold Bloom calls his list of the 13 indispensable writers 'a list of the life-saving equipment for western civilization: if we lose it, we won't survive". Ibsen as a life-raft seems able to float by himself, at any given moment he's being performed on a stage somewhere around the world. All the same, equipment like this has to be looked after, and we need to know where it is. This little book of 12 Afterwords by living Norwegian writers is a contribution to helping to keep the life-saving equipment in good shape.

Bjarne Buset
Press Office
Gyldendal Norsk Forlag

AFTERWORD TO *BRAND*

by Hanne Ørstavik

What is it about *Brand*? For a number of years I've been preoccupied with it. When restlessness overwhelms me and I can't sit still and read any longer, then I take my talking-book[1] tapes of *Brand* out into the wood. I have a number of talking books, but it's *Brand* I take with me. Time after time. And there I walk, walk and walk and listen to *Brand*.

> *Oh, how greatly I long*
> *For light and sun and gentleness,*
> *For the churchly silence of peace*
> *For life's lovely summers!* [2]

Brand says this at the very end. But it is actually what he is saying all the time, throughout the play. During, inside. He just cannot do it. He wants it to be good, he himself wants to be good. And for Brand, what is good is what is right.

> *Life's divided from the Word and the Faith*
> *No-one cares enough to Be.* [3]

---

1   Henrik Ibsen: *Brand*. NRK Radioteateret og Lydbokforlaget, 1999.
2   Henrik Ibsen: *Brand. Et dramatisk dikt*. First published in 1866. The page references given are for the paperback version published by Gyldendal Norsk Forlag in 2001.
3   p. 21

He wants live in accord with what he himself believes in and stands for. But what is it that *is* right? When you stand there, in the middle of all that is happening to you? When, for example, there's a storm blowing on the fjord and a woman arrives from the other side to fetch the priest. She says that they were starving and the youngest child began to scream, so her husband beat the child to death. Then he tried to take his own life. Now he lies there, unshriven, daring neither to live nor die, as Ibsen writes. But he is actually dying and that is why she has come, to fetch the priest, so her husband can be forgiven his sins and die in peace. But the road round the fjord has been closed by an avalanche. And no one wants to cross the fjord in the storm. They dare not risk their life. And the woman whose husband is dying won't get in the boat either, she has her children to think of, if she dies they have no one.

Then Brand gets into the boat. Brand trusts that the crossing is in God's hands, for what God does is good. Whatever. However. That's what it says in the Bible. That we must give everything up unto God. And Brand wants to do that, he wants to lean on God, to be held. And he leans. And the boat is carried over the fjord.

The desperate thing about all this is that we also understand the woman, the mother, who does not go in the boat, her reasons for not doing so. Yes, with all our heart we also understand her, the other children she's thinking of, who are sitting there

> *staring big-eyed,*
> *huddled together*
> *fledglings by the chimney corner*
> *those who only watched –.*[4]

But the boat makes it over. Everything is alright. This time everything is alright. Brand got there and talked to the husband and heard his confession. But was it right?

How can we live a life where what we do is right and at the same time good?

How to live?

4   p. 38

In the play – *Brand* – I ponder this question, time after time. There is the sheriff, who looks after his own patch. Oh, how I recognise that, here and now, today. The evasion of responsibility, the good excuses. Oh, how we look after our own patch. I do it too. That's just it. I am Brand. But I am also the sheriff. And I am the mother of the children there in the cottage. I am those children. And I am Agnes who laughs in the heather at Einar's side, on the way over the mountain, light-footed, to the fjord. I am her just as much then, as when she is drawn to Brand, to the weight in him.

I have them all within me. I know them as voices within me, voices that struggle within me. And I know the struggle of Brand. That is why I read and listen to this play over and over again, to be in it, to be in this struggle, for it to be kept open. For the struggle is not resolved, it is always there, it is ongoing, in our life, in our society. All the time. Who am I? Who do I want to be? How to live with the others, how to make sense of things, how to get it right?

I notice that it is not God who interests me when I read Brand. But questions about God are there, in the text, everywhere. Where is God? What is God? Is there any God? What the text shows does exist, is us. You and I. We exist, at least. And what do we do? What should we do with each other? And with ourselves?

And then there's the riddle of Brand that I am drawn to. The human being, Brand. His hardness, his unbending principles. That which makes him great and destructive, at the same time. That which makes him reject his mother's request to come to her as she lies dying. He cannot. He simply cannot. And when his own son is about to die, Brand can save him by moving away from the village, out of the shadow and the damp cold to a more sunny place, but he does not. And his son dies. He could have prevented it, he is about to do so, almost, almost, and I want him to do it, each time I read it, I cry out: yes Brand, yes, move! But then it's as if something turns in him and he doesn't do it. What is it that turns? Why? This hardness in him, what is it? Where does it come from? And perhaps most of all, how can it change?

His obduracy, his hardness and his strictness, how can it change? Will it ever change? Isn't that what we're waiting for, the whole time we are reading *Brand*, all the way, that it will change?

But at the same time, can it change, without being lost? What Brand believes in, what he stands for. Does he have to give this up to be able to live with others?

Die! The world has no use for you![5]

And yet:

The one can give light to the many.[6]

In the tension between these two extremes, stands Brand. To live, to be true. That is what he is sent to do, not because he wants to, but because he must. There is something in Brand that must do this.[7]

And when I read Brand, I don't see this drive in him, this fire, as cold and authoritarian. That is the way it becomes, the way it works, cold and hard, in relation to others, to living life, reality. But the play is important because it shows the struggle of someone who believes. Believes and believes. Wants to believe, because he *must*. Oh yes, Brand believes in something and he fights for it. And then, at the very end, when he says

Jesus, I called out your name;
You never took me in your embrace;[8]

then I know that it is true. I know that what Brand really wanted was light and sun and gentleness. He yearned desperately for it. Yes, he has yearned, desperately. He has yearned for it to be true, so that the light of the truth might warm his soul, so that it was good and not destructive. But that's not the way it turned out. Has he not been heard? Or has he not made it? We could say that he had his chance, but he did not take it. Why not? Why did they not move to another village and save the child? Brand could not. But why could he not?

Because *Jesus* never took him in his embrace? But what does that mean?

Brand did get Agnes. Agnes heard him and held him. She has rocked and comforted and supported him, stood by. But it does not

---

5   p. 177
6   p. 177
7   p. 176
8   p. 180

feed Brand's longing, it does not fill him. The place Brand cries out from is so desolate and empty, he is all alone there. No other human being can get through there. Not even God.

But this is not about some ultimate definition of God. No, it is always about Brand, Brand's struggle, his compulsion. The cry, the cry for an answer, to be embraced and held, in all he is. And maybe only something greater than ourselves can bear that cry, hear it, answer? For that is how huge that cry sometimes seems. But then how best to live? When there is no reply from up above?

And Brand has a lot. As the sheriff says to him:

> *You own the riches of the world,*
> *Are heirs to a mother's wealth,*
> *You have a child to live for,*
> *A beloved wife; – the chance of happiness*
> *Offered you as by a gentle hand![9]*

but there is this other thing – that he *must*. He must and he must and he must. He can do nothing else:

> *Myself I lose if I should retreat[10]*

And it is here, into this, that Brand digs and stands alone. In the play and in me. In this desperation, this feeling that he will disappear if he gives way. What is he to do? He can do nothing else. Do nothing other than say no to his mother who lies dying, to remain in the village, where his son dies. He can do nothing else. Even though he really wants to. He wants to do what is good. And what is good is right. So he does what is right, which is sharp and hard. But it does not become good. No, it does not.

Because Brand does not open himself. He clings on. In order not to disappear. And no-one, not even God, God in Agnes, Agnes in God, God in the child, in the mother, no-one, no-one can warm him, can go deep enough. It does not get in, in to where something might melt, so that he can let go. So that he can finally let go of what he is holding and holding on to, so that he can open himself. For if some-

---

9   p. 76
10   p. 76

thing is to reach Brand, then he has to open himself to it. But how can he open himself?

At the end, at the very end, Brand weeps. And the tears he weeps are a crack, an opening through which something might just reach him. A way in to where something might move him, where something might change, where something might be released. But it is not until the penultimate page that he cries and then the avalanche comes that takes him, there are so many things that are too late. And Gerd asks the question that aches in me throughout the whole text: why did he not cry before?

This is what draws me, to see all this, to see the despair in this, and recognise it all. To recognise it all in me and yet have no answer, no solution. That is why I walk in the woods and listen to *Brand*. Not to be able to classify and fold it all neatly together, see it dealt with efficiently and sort it away. No, on the contrary, it is to be part of it. To be in it. To be in that cry, to be in Brand's cry and let it cry all through me.

– – –

Hanne Ørstavik was born in Finnmark in 1969. She is a writer and has published seven novels. *Presten* (The Priest), the most recent of these, was awarded the Brage Prize in 2004. She has also won a number of other literary prizes, including the Sult Prize and the Dobloug Prize, and her work has been translated into many languages.

RENTING WORLD CITIZENSHIP

Afterword to *Peer Gynt* by Thomas Hylland Eriksen

Peer Gynt has no fear of globalisation. He is the only EU supporter in the village and in his opinion it's quite alright for WTO to support certain principles that regulate international trading, provided it doesn't entail any loss for him and it will in practise be possible to break the rules. Which is always the case. The adaptable and unscrupulous man will always find a loophole. Peer Gynt is an unfocused enthusiast. He personifies the attitude that Nietzsche, some twenty years later, would describe as 'active nihilism'. He wants everything, but not what he's got.

When he appeared in 1867, Peer had no direct predecessor in literature. He does share certain characteristics with Goethe's Faust and is related to the *trickster* of folk stories, in Norway known as the Ash Lad and in West Africa as Anansi or the spider. But there is something undeniably new and fresh, powerful in an almost animal way and not least, something disturbing about Peer Gynt. That power remains intact after nearly one and a half centuries of performances in various languages, countless analyses and learned readings. Neither its verse form nor its frequently local colouring have proved a hindrance for the character Peer Gynt and he speaks as directly to people in the 21st century as he did to his own contemporaries.

The 1860s were every bit as turbulent as our own times. The industrial revolution brought with it both affluence and poverty. New cities grew up and the older ones became both bigger and more crowded. The whole population structure of the North Atlantic countries changed. There was large-scale emigration to North America from the poorest parts of Europe; millions of people put the past behind them, severed their roots and made a fresh start. Secularisation got under way. Before – and especially after – the year of revolutions in 1848, new ideas, socialism and nationalism, began to spread. Darwin's theory of evolution made it possible for educated people to declare themselves godless. Yet the strongest ideological impulse was Manchester liberalism. This ideology bore remarkable similarities to the so-called new liberalism of our own times, being a combination of the deregularisation of the economy, the opening of the public sector to competition, a global market, the de-ideologisation of politics and strong promotion of notions of individual freedom.

Both new and old liberalism share a global orientation and preach the blessings of free trade. Both make mantric use of the concept of freedom and accuse all those in favour of limitations on trade of being opposed to freedom. (That the rich countries in practise protect their own activities is another matter – they are in favour of trading, but not importing.) And back then, as now, few of the pillars of society wished it to be said of them that they were opposed to freedom.

Both Manchester and new liberalism encourage personalities like Peer Gynt. In the 1860s, however, such characters were probably rarities in Norwegian communities. Impulses from the wider world travelled more slowly in those days, especially inland; in addition, most people were attached to the family and the farm. Peer Gynt, only in his twenties, was already an outsider in the community, admired, feared and despised. He was a faithless seducer of women, an irresponsible pleasure-seeker who ran off into the mountains rather than help his mother with the harvest, a liar and a boaster. The only woman in the village who supports him comes from a politically weak family of new arrivals who, moreover, are limited by protestant scruples concerning duty and loyalty.

In our times, an age characterised by the democratised potential for self-expression that has been forced through over a long and strenuous twentieth century, anyone who chooses can try the Peer Gynt way. But first they ought to read the play, for if they do they will realise that, while new liberalism offers great freedom and great scope, it has little to offer when the hard times come. Peer 'does not die in the middle of the Fifth Act', but he might perhaps wish he had done so.

So Peer makes full use of the values associated with individual freedom. But let's go one step further and ask, can Peer also be used to
symbolise the rootless cosmopolitan? It might be interesting to hear
Salman Rushdie's views on the matter. The British-Indian nationless
Rushdie has, after all, in all his writing, cultivated rootlessness and
the freedom to choose where and whether to belong or not. He re-
gards the conforming pressures of religion and culture as a merciless
form of compulsion. The dilemma is, all the same, that if one chooses
freedom then perhaps one rejects security at the same time and if
one chooses self-realisation, then perhaps one is also rejecting the
option to care about others.

Researchers on the nature of national identities have discussed
the so-called 'potato principle': wherever potatoes (or whatever else)
are cultivated, people put down deep roots and become susceptible
to national romanticism and the reactionary cultivation of the home.
The potato cultivators (or whatever else) are no longer the majority in Norway, but as long as the belief persists that they are, then
nationalism continues to be operative. Here we find Rushdie's polar
opposite, and for most the conclusion is that the thing is to strike the
right balance.

Peer Gynt stands for the opposite of the potato principle. The First
Act introduces him as a contrary man, marching to the sound of his
own drum: he is an irresponsible man who neglects his obligations,
a passionate seducer who respects neither religion, women, nor the
accepted values of his society. He is an adventurer who does not fit in
with the well-regulated community's routine existence. We prick up
our ears particularly when some dissonance becomes apparent in the
midst of all this self-assurance. The wedding scene shows us a man
who is weak-willed, in addition to everything else. He had intended
to stay sober, but all the same drinks when he's made to. Later in life,
problems always arise for him when he has been tempted and given
in. Usually women are involved.

Peer has power and charm, but he lacks direction. In his day, the
slave trade was officially abolished (in the French and British colo-
nies this happened in 1810) and good Christians were not supposed
to help the spread of competing religions. Yet he admits without
shame: "Most of my trade/was in blacks to Carolina/and fetishes to

China". It was where the easiest money was and a man like Peer will always tends to follow the path of least resistance.

When I read this scene, my thoughts inevitably turn to the 'yuppie' era of the 1980s, a time when a Gyntian version of morality was rapidly making its way into social democratic Norway and a new class of capitalist was emerging with no roots in the notion of creating social values. There is a story that one such capitalist once visited a factory in which he had bought a large number of shares. When the employees tried to show him what they were making, including porcelain toilet bowls, he is reported to have said: 'Toilets? I'm not interested in toilets! I'm interested in money!'

Peer has no long-term obligations, he is restricted neither by conscience nor guilt:

> The Gyntian self – it's that array
> Of wishes, hopes and desires, –
> The Gyntian self – it's that sea
> Of whims, challenges and demands,
> In short, all that which swells my chest
> And means that it is I who live.

The lack of a firm value system is the most provocative thing about Peer today, as it was back in the 19th century. For what is it that this man lives for, beyond excitement and the thrill of the moment? With no core to his personality, Peer is as receptive as a sponge to impulses from outside. In the Fourth Act, in which we meet an affluent, middle-aged, cosmopolitan Peer somewhere in Morocco, he carries on a worldly conversation with his dinner guests – a German, an Englishman, a Swede and a Frenchman. They are full of admiration for their hospitable and articulate host and the German, von Eberkopf, praises Peer for his tenancy of world citizenship. At one point the Frenchman, Monsieur Ballon, asks Peer: "You are Norwegian, aren't you?" To which Peer Gynt replies:

> By birth, indeed.
> But a world citizen by inclination.
> For the joys I have known
> I can thank America.
> The well-stacked library shelves

Are thanks to Germany's younger schools.
My waistcoat is from France,
From England I got the will to work
And an instinct for what was best for me.
The Jew has taught me how to wait,
A taste for the good things of life
Came my way from Italy,

Does this not resemble a pretty good defence of cultural globalisation? That it should be the amoral, unprincipled Peer Gynt who offers it might be problematic for those of us who view the global spread of cultures as a potentially valuable phenomenon. Throughout his adult life, Ibsen himself was contemptuous of the narrow nationalism and self-righteousness that infected Norwegian public life, then as now. He spent 27 years in voluntary exile, almost as long as Peer Gynt himself. But Peer Gynt forces us to consider the possibility that those who are most receptive to cultural influences from outside are perhaps those who have least to lose. What one stands to lose by copying the ways of others is oneself; but for those who have no self to lose, the problem is irrelevant. The answer is – fortunately – that there are a number of ways in which we can be influenced from without and the 'self' can have a core, even if it is a mosaic of digested impulses. Peer, on the other hand, seems to represent the opportunism that goes whichever way the wind blows, shunning above all else obligation. In this light, he is an eternally adolescent Peter Pan.

Another interpretation could be that Peer revolts not against the demand for moral integrity, but against the cultivation of sincerity. In contrast to his predecessor Brand, he does not care to examine 'the heart and the kidneys'. If he had had a morality, it would necessarily have involved the ethics of consistent behaviour rather than of temperament. But he is never burdened with any such thing. Bob Marley sang 'you can't run away from yourself', which presupposes that one has a self to run from. Peer's solution to the problems he encounters on his way through life is to run away from them, as far and as fast as he can. At the journey's end, he is not even considered worthy of a place in hell, as he has not been a conscious sinner, merely an opportunist who has spent his life surfing on the waves that happened to come his way.

Just to avoid any confusion: I do not think that *Peer Gynt* should be read as a study in the psychological aspects of liberal economic theory. But grant at least that it is one possible interpretation! We might put it like this: following this play, Ibsen abandoned not only the verse form, but also the themes associated with national romanticism. Directly after the Mountain King has delivered his final line about his intention to travel to the city – 'I'm off to the theatre. It says in the paper they're looking for nationalist subject matter – ', Ibsen moves on to the so-called 'plays on contemporary life'. What is remarkable is that *Brand* and *Peer Gynt* seem now to have a greater relevance than plays like *A Doll's House, The Pillars of Society* and *Ghosts*. It is not an inhibited, mildly syphilitic middle-class, mentally and socially crippled, which characterises our age, but rather the tensions between the fundamentalist politics of identity (based on nation, religion or some other criterion) and a yea-saying hedonism that lives for the pleasures of the moment. It is the conflict between Peer Gynt and Brand that is now playing on the stage of contemporary life.

In defence of the superficial version of the cosmopolitan attitude, one might observe that, while a great deal can be said about Peer, he will never become a fascist. A fellow-traveller perhaps – possibly in the same sense as Johan Borgen's Lillelord – but one cannot envisage him as a fanatic. When social anthropologist Marianne Gullestad was asked if it was not worrying that Peer Gynt seemed to be a role model for today's Norwegian leaders, her response was that we should be relieved it was not Brand instead. Seen in this light, a factor of some significance is that, with the exception of women and death, only the Great Bøyg is able to put the brakes on Peer – the state, in other words. Perhaps that also tells us something about new liberalism.

The most well-known scene in the Fifth Act shows an old Peer on the night before Whitsun gathering onions. He has lost all he owned in the shipwreck and had a few jolting encounters with death. In other words he is now given over to brooding about life and sits there, peeling an onion as though it were his personality and the sum of his life's wisdom he is penetrating. The conclusion is unavoidable: 'Goodness, how many layers!/ Surely the core's near now?'

The frightening, but perhaps also liberating, realisation that there is no core to be uncovered has been a source of inspiration to social anthropologists right up to our own times. The influential thinker, Zygmunt Bauman, uses it as a leitmotif that runs through much of his writing, which concerns itself with the unstable nature of modern people and the lack of roots. He is not unequivocally negative in his response to this tendency, but makes the point that freedom has a price, which is the loss of security. In a book about 'new working life' in the field of consultancies and the information industry, *The Flexible Person,* the sociologist Richard Sennett describes the post-modern careerist as the information consultants and corporate lawyers who spend far too much of their time at airports, with their computers in their laps, and who long for a core, something firm and predictably routine, such as their parents had in their modest occupations as bakers, or perhaps janitors.

Peer has 'lived as a mountain troll, an egoist who is 'himself, and that'll do' and the Button Moulder explains to him that he therefore must be melted down and recast. But he is also a fascinating person. Even if they do not achieve anything of lasting value, it is people like Peer who get things moving in the world. And people with a touch of Peer are still to be found, thank goodness. When the celebrated peace scholar and restless globetrotter, Johan Galtung, celebrated his 70th birthday in 1998, the ageing peace activist, Eva Nordland, sat down at the piano and performed 'Solveig's Song'. It was intended to reflect the division of work between the two of them – 'John Lackland' had conquered the world, while she stayed at home – but it was also a declaration of love for the uninhibited, immodest and frenetic extroversion which the celebrant shares with the man behind the debatable statement, 'I've seen it in black and white – and the truth is plain – no man's a prophet in his own land.'

Peer Gynt is the opposite of the kind of sterling and predictable person upon whom one can rely. But, by way of compensation, he gives us all the more to talk about.

– – –

Thomas Hylland Eriksen is Professor of Social Anthropology at the University of Oslo and at Vrije University in Amsterdam. He also leads the research programme "Cultural complexity in the new Norway". He has published many different types of non-fiction books and one novel. Several of his books examine culture in Norway and multiculturalism. He has also written about Darwin, nationalism, globalisation and hard times.

WHAT HELMER SAID

Afterword to *A Doll's House* by Brit Bildøen

A hundred and twenty five years on …

An author's popularity is usually a variable thing. The writings can slumber for a while, until some accidental circumstance brings them to the interest and attention of other, newer eyes. But Ibsen has never slumbered. Both here and abroad, he has been constantly up and about. There are many good reasons for this. But there is perhaps one reason in particular why we never tire of *A Doll's House, Peer Gynt, The Wild Duck, Hedda Gabler* and all the others – and that is that the characters in his plays are always searching for the truth in one way or another. They are searching for their own centres and for the right way to live life. In the individualistic twentieth century that has just come to a close, this theme retained its appeal throughout. And what keeps Ibsen's dramas from stagnating, what enables them to be performed and experienced in constantly new ways, is that Ibsen, whose characters are engaged in a more or less desperate search for the truth, did not himself try to provide it. In a letter (in rhyme!) to Brandes in 1875 he wrote: "I prefer to ask; my call is not to answer!" This was not some fancy aphorism, but a conviction with which Ibsen managed to invest all his literary activity. The truths in his plays are manifold and one has to discover them for oneself. The truths are changeable, according to the light in which one sees the plays. The light of history, the director's particular choice of emphasis, our own personal ballast – all these elements play a part. Was Nora right to leave Helmer? Where did she go? What did she mean by 'the most wonderful thing?' we ask, and if we want the answer then we are compelled to look inwards.

Of all those for whom *A Doll's House* has been important, it has first and foremost been so for the half of the world's population that calls itself woman. *A Doll's House* has played a large part in the biggest political movement of the last hundred years, the women's liberation movement. Nora's revolt against a man who did not value her as a person and a social system that allowed women very little room to manoeuvre, has become an act of considerable symbolic value. For one hundred and twenty-five years now, Nora's line "First and foremost, I am a person" has been a mantra for legions of women. But attempts to cast Helmer simply as *the bad guy* and Nora as *the good girl* have not always been so easy, except perhaps during the 1970s. The characters are quite simply too human to allow this. This is another aspect of Ibsen's talent, another reason why he and the characters he created have become immortal. He created complex characters and tightened his plots into intricate knots that no-one ever quite manages to unravel.

Nora and Helmer in the 70s

In several interviews, Liv Ullmann has related a telling story from the time she played Nora on Broadway in 1975. This was the golden era of women's lib and Nora was the great heroine, while Sam Waterston, who played Helmer, was having a difficult time arousing enthusiasm for his character. During the final rehearsals, which were played before an audience, he was actually given the bird. Waterston was greatly distressed by this and did not wish to continue. So, before the final dress rehearsal, Ullmann suggested that they do yoga to build up his resolve. In the process, he strained his ankle and had to enter the stage using a stick. This proved to be the answer, for now the whistling and booing stopped. And when Waterston graduated to crutches at the premier, it silenced even the applause when Nora left him. The woman's triumph paled slightly, when the man she was leaving was left disabled at home. So harsh was the light cast by history in the 1970s that it was necessary for the role of Helmer to be played by an actor on crutches.

It has probably never been difficult to see Nora and Helmer as products of a rigid social structure, as actors in carefully control-led role-play. Nora's roles in the marriage are lark, squirrel, and – of course – doll. Helmer's roles are domestic tyrant and master. He has also taken it upon himself to represent Commonsense and Modera-tion. Both are imprisoned by this system, which exploits human be-ings just as it exploits women. But are they all dolls? Helmer too? Or is Helmer the puppet-master who makes them all dance: Nora, Dr Rank, Krogstad and Fru Linde? There is much to suggest that he has always understood the warmth of Dr Rank's feelings for Nora, but has allowed them to carry on with their flirtatious game-play-ing. And it turns out that Helmer is every bit as much in Krogstad's power as vice-versa. Helmer leads, but he is also led. In Ibsen's plays the characters are seldom simply good or bad. Once again we are left with several possible answers and none of them are straightforward.

From squirrel to suffragette

There has always been disagreement about the last act, the leaving scene itself and the decisive discussion between Nora and Helmer. Many have criticised the scene on the grounds that Nora wakes up so suddenly. Throughout the whole play she has presented herself as diz-zy and naive, but here she is suddenly transformed into an Amazon:

Helmer. It's so distressing, the way you betray your most sacred obligations.

Nora. What do you consider to be my most sacred obligations?

Helmer. You mean I even have to tell you that! Aren't they the obligations you have towards your husband and your children?

Nora. I have other obligations which are just as sacred.

Helmer. No you do not. What obligations might *they* be?

Nora. My obligations to myself.

Helmer. You are first and foremost a housewife and a mother.

Nora. I don't believe that anymore. I believe that I am first and foremost a person, myself, just as you are – or at least I should try to be that.

Many find that Nora's eyes open a little too quickly here and that Ibsen too obviously uses her as a mouthpiece for his own views – or for the ideas in vogue at the time. Has he taken a shortcut here and jumped over a stage or two of Nora's development? Or was there really another woman behind the one we and Helmer had learnt to know all the time? A stronger and more dangerous woman than the one whose rebellion consists of nibbling macaroons in secret? Nora hangs on desperately, she tries to sustain the child within as long as she can. But it turns out that she is also very moral and hard when the time comes. Whatever one makes of this sudden turn in the play, there has been a major upheaval within a very short space of time. In just a few short words, Helmer has declassified Nora and understandably she reacts to this violently. What we witness in this last meeting between Nora and Helmer are two people who abruptly lose their innocence. It is inevitable that the gulf of self-insight and understanding that opens up between them must have consequences.

In her memoir, *Changing*, Liv Ullmann relates that her Nora several times, perhaps as often as ten times, burst out 'Oh, I'm so happy'. She chose to let Nora say this without joy and the last time in great desperation and anxiety. One critic commented that she was helping out Ibsen – so that the break in the final act would not come so suddenly. Several devices have been used to prepare the audience for the change in Nora in the final act – the play permits this. Nora's wildness as she dances the tarantella can function as such a device. Here she expresses feelings for which – as yet – there are no words. Perhaps the tarantella accelerates the process of maturation in Nora. Wordlessly, she approaches the madness and fear that are part of her project. And acquires the strength to carry it out. She awakes from her 'sleeping princess' role and goes, leaving Helmer behind with his crutches.

Nora and Helmer in China

Agnete Haaland had a similar and yet very different experience when she played Nora in a Chinese version of *A Doll's House* in 1997. Usually, when the audience was predominantly young, Nora's lines were greeted with assenting cheers. Older audiences, on the other hand, expressed loud sympathy with Helmer. But in this production, the Chinese Helmer had studied in the West and taken a Norwegian Nora home to China with him. Thus the conflict between Nora and

Helmer is not just about the marriage, it is also a cultural collision between a western woman and Helmer, who stands for the old China. Here the man is still head of the household and losing face is the worst thing that can happen. Seen in this light, Nora's financial acrobatics are evidence of a western woman's lack of respect for the native culture, something that does great harm to her husband. So there were many in the audience who gave a sigh of relief when Nora picked up her suitcase and candlestick – a western symbol! – and went out the door. Seen from another perspective, Nora was revolting against the old order. And since she was rebelling against authority, it could also be interpreted as a revolt against Mao – even if unspoken. And in that case, it is conceivable that there is a use for her out there, which is another reason why the *young* audiences cheered Nora when she left. So, no tears for Nora's exit in China!

Interviewed in *Bergens Tidende*, the play's director, Liu Tiegang, recalled the importance of Ibsen in his life and how he had actually risked his life for Ibsen in the days of the Cultural Revolution. During the 1960s, he and a friend broke into a library, because they had heard rumours that all the books were to be sent to the paper mill for recycling. There he found two sets of Ibsen's Collected Works, which he kept hidden throughout the whole Cultural Revolution. A reading of *An Enemy of the People*, he relates, made it clear to him that Ibsen was not a reactionary, but a man with Leftist sympathies.

The naughty macaroons

Ibsen is regarded as a supporter of the women's movement, a view which he sought to modify. Invited to attend a women's conference in Christiania in 1898, he thanked the speakers for their words of praise, but declined the honour of consciously having worked to promote the women's movement. 'My task has been the description of what is human', he insisted. His Nora became a symbol of women's liberation, but Ibsen was above all concerned with the fact that people seemed to lack the will or the opportunity to live a life in truth and freedom. And in Ibsen's day, it was women who were particularly affected by this condition. On one point, however, the dramatist was clear: without truth there can be no change and no real freedom. And as previously noted, in his plays it is often the truth that must be brought out into the open. But he does not preach, nor does he 'psychologise'; what he does is articulate the individual's situation in a given context. His use of the phrase 'a tragedy of contemporary life' for the first draft of *A Doll's House* indicates that Ibsen himself intended to stress the fact that the play ought to be understood in the light of the historical moment in which it was conceived. And yet time and again we see that it is possible to breathe new and contemporary life into this play, and to change its social and temporal conditions. One of the questions raised by Ibsen's realist dramas is whether we still live in the same type of bourgeois society today, one which places restrictions on us and makes us unfree.

Among the most distressing scenes in the play is the 'macaroon scene', in which Helmer reduces Nora to a state of complete infantility:

Helmer (wags his finger). Little sweet-tooth didn't let herself go in town today now, did she?

Nora. No, whatever makes you say that!

Helmer. So little sweet-tooth really didn't make a tiny detour to the baker's shop?

Nora. No, Torvald, honestly, I promise you –

Helmer. Not been at the jam?

Nora. No, absolutely not.

Helmer. Not even nibbled at a macaroon or two?

Nora. No, Torvald, I promise you, honestly –

Helmer. Hey hey hey – it's only my little joke –

Nora (approaches the table on the right). It would never occur to me to do anything that would displease you.

Here Nora has just sneaked a macaroon and brushed the crumbs away. It's silly of her, of course, but even worse of him to carry on the way he does. And while we're thinking this, perhaps we're also thinking that, well, thank goodness we don't behave like that today! But hang on … is that really true? Today women hide their impulse buys at the back of the wardrobe, so that when the time finally comes to wear the new jacket or use the new bag they can say – Oh but I bought that ages ago! Even today, it seems, Helmer is being manipulated. But what part do macaroon scenes like these play in Norwegian homes now that most women have achieved economic independence? There is no easy answer. But there is much to suggest that there are still battles to be won.

Ibsen recognised this need for freedom and for elbow room, and he managed to communicate it to others. In his notes to *A Doll's House* he wrote that there are 'two kinds of spiritual law, two kinds of conscience, one in men and a quite different one in women'. His conscience drove him to create characters with many nuances in his plays. Ibsen depicted complex – and thereby very human – characters. This was particularly true of his women, which was extraordinary in those days. Even today it should not be taken forgranted …

"The most wonderful thing"

The key phrase, 'the most wonderful thing', has counterparts in several of Ibsen's plays – for example 'the thing which cannot be said' in *The Lady from the Sea*. In these plays, abstract and enigmatic periphrases are allowed to express what the main characters cannot say directly in words. These words form a kind of kernel in the plays, or rather black holes around which all else gravitates. Ibsen gives us an indirect glimpse into what is going on inside the characters, their darkest, deepest, strongest feelings and desires. We can discuss endlessly what Nora meant when she wished for 'the most wonderful thing'. And what is implied when, at the very end, Helmer voices the same words.

Ibsen gives us a pretty clear indication of what Nora means by the expression. For her, 'the most wonderful thing' would be proof that Helmer had become the strong and good husband she deep down hopes and believes he can be. She wants proof that he is worthy of her love and the sacrifice she has made in borrowing the money to save his health. In order to borrow this money, Nora forged her father's signature – something which gives the lawyer, Krogstad, power over the couple. When he impresses upon Nora the gravity of what she has done, her hope is that Helmer will see that her intentions were good and will take it as a declaration of love. For Helmer, these same words probably express the wish to have Nora back, at least, at the moment he says them. But there is a chance they will acquire a greater resonance for him too, if he only allows them to continue resounding in his head for a while longer.

There has been a great deal of discussion about Nora's possible fate after the door slams, some of it rather fanciful. In her 1979 play, *What happened after Nora had left her husband, or the pillars of society*, the Nobel prizewinner, Elfriede Jelinek, depicted a Nora who undergoes a process of self-proletarisation and ends up a sex-slave. Some directors have Nora turning back on the steps, others have her shooting Helmer. When Mao started the Long March in China in 1935, it was clear to Chinese audiences that Nora left Helmer in order to be one of Mao's foot soldiers. Since then, 1935 has been known as 'Nora's year' in Chinese history books. One must also mention the fact that Ibsen wrote an alternative ending to the play, to prevent directors who could not live with Nora's 'impossible' choice from letting her stay in the house.

And what happens to Helmer? There are not nearly as many theories about this. Helmer too pays a high price. He played the game in the way he thought it was supposed to be played. In Beijing, older audiences sighed with relief as Nora walked out the door – finally, Helmer was free of this disturbing element in his life! In New York he was left behind, bewildered, on his crutches. Life as a single father is never going to be easy, no matter where and in what era Helmer finds himself.

What Helmer said

After what has happened, after the innocence is gone and the fateful words have fallen from Helmer's mouth, it is inconceivable that this relationship could continue. It would undermine Nora's position too much, now that the uncertainty of it has been openly articulated. Throughout the play, Nora has wondered about her own value and now, with a few simple words, Helmer lets her know what it is:

Helmer. (…) The matter must be hushed up, at any price. As for you and I, everything must appear to continue as normal. Naturally, this is only for public show. So you shall remain in this house – of course. But you will not be allowed to raise the children; I dare not entrust them to you –. (…)

How does one assess one's worth, one's status within a marriage? One measure might be the strength of one's position when the bad times come along. Nora and Helmer have had some good years – or at least so Helmer believes, blissfully ignorant of Nora's financial acrobatics and of the struggle she has had to pay back the loan. Now, suddenly, the bad days are here. Incredibly, everything Helmer has believed in, everything that seemed to be settled and secure, is on the verge of disappearing at any moment.

Helmer (paces the floor). Oh what a terrible awakening. In all these eight years, she was my light and my pride. A hypocrite and a liar. Worse, worse – a criminal! Oh the fathomless, hideous depths of it all. Terrible. Terrible.

Even after the letter has arrived from a remorseful Krogstad and the danger has passed, and Helmer is congratulating himself on having forgiven Nora, she cannot live with the knowledge that she could be rubbed out of the story so easily. It is impossible for her to remain in a house where such degradation might occur at any time, simply by Helmer opening his mouth. Words spoken in fathomless despair and anxiety must be deemed to be as truthful as those spoken in a mood of optimism and happiness. Or just as untruthful. And when one cannot act in accordance with either, neither words spoken in love, nor those uttered in disgust, then what remains? This insight leads to another revelation for Nora: she has never been happy in Helmer's house – 'merely cheerful'. The false foundations of the marriage are revealed to her in all their horror. Everything has been a game, there is no room in their married life for what is right and truthful. And now the pilot with whom Nora has navigated all these years has suddenly disqualified himself as her guiding light. Helmer does not improve matters when he implies that the episode will serve to increase the sense that she is his property. He believes that when a man has forgiven his wife with all his heart, then she : ' ...thereby becomes his property in a twofold sense; he has so to speak re-admitted her to the world, she becomes as it were both his wife and his child (…)'

After this, Nora can trust only herself. In the course of a single evening she has grown up; she can no longer allow herself to be treated like a child. Nor can she accept that it is Helmer, with his wavering array of attitudes, who is to decide the nature of her relationship with her children. That is why she has to go. If she remains with Helmer, one thing is certain and that is that 'the most wonderful thing' will never come about. If, on the other hand, she leaves, the possibility remains that both of them, one day, might experience this wonderful thing, individually, or together. The bare fact of Nora's leaving is tragic, but it carries with it a germ of hope.

Ibsen might agree that society is to blame, but he is clear about where the responsibility lies: it lies with the individual. This morality is very present in *A Doll's House*, where Nora recognises her responsibility, takes it seriously and leaves. She is not, like Peer Gynt, tempted by the Bøyg to go round the obstacles. If she pretends that what Helmer said was never said, then the rest of her life would be a bigger or more obvious lie than the one she realises she has been living so far.

– – –

Brit Bildøen was born in 1962. She is a trained librarian and published *Bilde av menn* (Pictures of Men), her first collection of poems, in 1991. Since then she has published several collections of poetry, children's books, novels and translations of poetry. She has also worked as a literary consultant and critic. Bildøen is currently the senior literary consultant at Det norske Samlaget publishing house, and an advisor on the creative writing course at the Litterär Gestaltning in Gothenburg. Her most recent publication is the novel *Alt som er* (All that is) (2004).

AFTERWORD TO *GHOSTS*

by Tore Rem

You don't win the Nobel Prize for writing *Ghosts*. At least, you didn't win it for writing something like that in Ibsen's lifetime. In this play the already world-famous dramatist went further than ever before. He marched straight into the inner sanctum of his society. And when the reader followed the play's characters through the fog and rain and darkness of the text, it was only to see these 'light-fearers' confronted with a merciless sun. Ibsen managed to write a play of great destructive power. In our encounters with a text that was elected to the literary canon a long, long time ago, it is easy to forget that *Ghosts* must be reckoned among the satanic verses of our literature.

The Nobel Prize has become one of literature's most efficient mechanisms for canonisation, yet its powers were never used on Ibsen. In his will, Alfred Nobel stipulated that the literary prize should go to someone who 'in the field of literature has produced the most idealistically inspired work'. And in the first decades of the prize's life, the Swedish Academy conscientiously carried out Nobel's last wish, in its own conservative interpretation of what that might be. Ibsen's most notorious play could hardly be said to have been 'idealistically inspired'. When his name came up for discussion in 1902, the Swedish Academy instead concentrated on his 'negativity and enigmatic qualities'. Ibsen had, quite simply, revolted against the norms that the Nobel Committee regarded as their own.

By the time *Ghosts* was published in 1881, Ibsen seems already to have been secure in the belief that the future belonged to him – and to his latest play. 'The minority is always right', he wrote to the Danish critic, Georg Brandes, a phrase that would recur in his next play, *An Enemy of the People*. And he told his Danish publisher, Gyldendal's Frederik V. Hegel, that 'the future belongs to my book. These chaps who are all in a lather about it can't even relate to their own contemporary reality'. Literary history, he assured his publisher, would hand down a crushing verdict on the critics of his work.

Ibsen was in tune with the future. He regarded himself as a 'spiritual pioneer'. We have long been used to hearing such observations about the author and his work. But for precisely that reason it might be worth while pausing a moment, to ask a few questions. Such as, precisely which future was Ibsen thinking of? And, what becomes of someone who invests so much in being ahead of the game, in escaping from his own time, when the front lines have advanced beyond his outposts and the former 'pioneer' is himself left behind? Instead of unconditionally accepting Ibsen's own self-judgement, it might be useful to place Ibsen and his text in their contemporary context.

Ibsen was never again as avant-garde as he was in *Ghosts*. At least, not according to his own understanding of frontier-fighting. In the wake of the negative early reactions, the anxious author contacted Hegel to enquire whether 'all this fuss' had harmed the sales of the book. And he wrote to a Swedish correspondent that he dared not go any further than he had done with *Ghosts*: 'A writer must not risk removing himself so far from his people that understanding is no longer possible.' In other words, at least the contemporary, as well as the future.

Despite the fact that Amalie Skram, in her review of *Ghosts*, placed Ibsen on another planet, she also felt that the play was about the present: 'This is not something we can push to one side. We know quite well that it is about our own times.' Just by openly taking as his theme questions about syphilis, genetic heritage, 'living in sin', incest and freethinking, by equating fallen women with fallen men, by questioning family, parental authority and religion, Ibsen declared both a belonging and a rejection. In terms of form as well, it is the most tightly structured of all Ibsen's plays. *Ghosts* broke with the 19th century theatre's preoccupation with the spectacular, tension and action. There is little action here and a great deal of talk. Slowly, mercilessly, inexorably, Ibsen strips bare the past, in order to – among other things – study and explain the characters' development, as well as show the motives for their words and deeds. Contemporary critics found this retrospective technique so striking that they returned to the theatre of antiquity, and Sophocles' *Oedipus Rex* in particular, to find its like. The comparison captured one aspect of Ibsen's dramaturgical method, at the same time as it allowed a useful connection to be made between a radical writer and the authors of antiquity. Ibsen had created a fatalistic drama for a new age, one in which biology and psychology took over the role of the gods.

With a few exceptions – chiefly Georg Brandes, Bjørnstjerne Bjørnson and Amalie Skram (who wrote in *Dagbaldet* as "ie" and who was then Amalie Müller) – *Ghosts* was given a slaughtering without parallel in Scandinavian literary history. None of the three main Scandinavian theatres offered to perform it. The critic, Henrik Jæger, in his reader's report for the Christiania Theatre, regretted that drama's powers to improve had been here replaced by 'pathological sensationalism', and suggested that one might as well open the National Hospital to the public 'for a suitable entrance fee'. And when, the following year, the Norwegian Parliament debated a request from Ibsen to have his annual writer's subsidy increased, one member expressed his satisfaction at the fact that books like *Ghosts* were published in Denmark and not in Norway: 'I note with pleasure that they bear a foreign land as their place of origin. And, I may add, such books should have no home here.'

Things were not much better in the country of publication. The censor at the Royal Theatre, Ibsen's main Scandinavian stage, dismissed *Ghosts* as a play that made 'a disgusting pathological phenomenon into the main element of the plot', and said that its effect was 'overwhelmingly degenerative'. As a result, the play did not become part of the Royal Theatre's repertoire until 1903. If we exclude a performance by some Scandinavians in Chicago and a number of other Midwest towns in 1882, the Swede, August Lindberg, was the first to give *Ghosts* a chance on the stage. The production visited all the Nordic capitals in 1883. Later, in the 1880s, came German productions by the Duke of Meiningen's group and Freie Bühne in Berlin. The Parisian group, Théâtre Libre, followed suit shortly afterwards.

So *Ghosts* rapidly became an international – or at least a European – phenomenon. And this phenomenon was not only controversial, it was subject to censorship. This was at a time when the theatre was often strictly controlled, with a local or government censor responsible for permitting or banning a performance. The furious reactions aroused by *Ghosts* can perhaps best be illustrated by the play's reception in the English-speaking world, specifically Great Britain, where it did not have its premier until ten years after its publication in Copenhagen.

An Anglo-Dutch producer, J.M. Grein, had for some time entertained hopes of establishing an alternative stage for new and experimental drama in London. His Independent Theatre was established in 1891 and it seemed to him that Ibsen's *Ghosts* would make a suitable opening. Informally, however, he was given a clear message by the theatre censor: 'No Ibsen here, please'. The solution was to find a loophole in the censorship law and that involved redefining the theatre as a private club. On 13 March 1891, the theatre gave *Ghosts* its British premier. The ensuing scandal seems to have exceeded all the producer's expectations.

Clement Scott of the *Daily Telegraph*, the leading critic of his day, called the performance 'an open sewer, a hideous untreated wound, a filthy act performed in public, a lepers' hospital with all its windows and doors wide open'. And in conclusion he appealed to public opinion, assisted if necessary by the law, to ensure that honest and decent citizens be properly shielded from exposure to such things. A horde of critics competed with similarly abusive reviews and for some time afterwards Ibsen was the most talked-about dramatist in Great Britain. In 1891 alone, one of the great 'Ibsen years' in England, hundreds of articles and reviews were devoted to him in the British press. *Ghosts* became an issue of domestic political concern. The theatre censor liased closely with the Home Secretary and for a while the matter threatened to become a subject of debate in the House of Commons. So offensive was this Scandinavian import deemed to be that it was not until 1914, 33 years after publication, that the censor granted a licence for the play to be performed freely on British stages.

"Books that are banned attract more attention as ghosts than they would have done living; the writer who is gagged today is tomorrow hailed for having been gagged", writes the South African author, J.M. Coetzee, who has himself to a great extent operated under a regime of censorship. His use of the word 'ghosts' is, in the light of Ibsen's experience, apposite. Anticipating Coetzee's reasoning, when the play was eventually given its licence in 1914, one of the censor's advisors suggested that the play would have been forgotten already had it not been banned some twenty years earlier. Even though the history of the censorship of *Ghosts* does not entirely explain the play's enduring status, it provides compelling evidence of the powers to provoke that it once contained.

In the world of literary criticism and in the speeches of literati, it is usual to refer to the 'strangeness' of all great literature, a quality that always eludes us, but which we sense has something to do with aesthetics. But perhaps we ought sometimes to turn this argument on its head and ask, what if the literature that we call great and that occupies a place of honour in our western canon due to its aesthetic qualities, is for precisely that reason at risk of losing some of its 'strangeness'? In other words, what happens to a text that is accorded the dignity of being a 'classic', and is then read accordingly?

Classics, by definition, don't go away. They are texts that have an enduring relevance in any new context and in successive ages. But they can, by their very ubiquity, long since have ceased to challenge us and to challenge our values. They are perhaps more likely to assume a simple role as confirmation of everything we hold dear, of all we take pride in and identify ourselves with – a literature tamed by culture. Probably no Norwegian writer provides a better example of this than Ibsen.

The canonisation of certain texts can, in other words, have a harmonising function. It can make us treat texts that are very different from each other as being more alike than they actually warrant. We stress the universality of their values, we equip them with our own 'idealistic direction' and with that we give them an edifying function in our theatres, schools and universities, as well as in our national mythology. Applying this to *Ghosts*, we can, for example, define the play as documenting what is, historically speaking, a progressive movement and as a testament to an author who showed us the way to ourselves. So we can, if we continue to think against the grain, regard *Ghosts* as the celebration of ourselves as the victors of history.

But then what is left of those aspects of the play that really ought to challenge us today? That ought to shake us out of our complacency and cause us to think deeply about our own situation? How much remains now of the power that *Ghosts* once contained for its contemporary audiences and readers?

'Ibsen is always relevant.' This is one of the most monumental clichés about Norwegian literature. The likelihood of Ibsen being 'just as relevant' today as he was in 1881 is hardly great. If he is 'relevant', then it must presumably be in new ways. And come to think of it, what does it mean to be 'relevant'? And how is this relevance distinct from the simple status of being 'classic'?

Might it not be more fruitful to approach Ibsen as our non-contemporary? It is after all quite possible – and in line with the idea of the dead 'walking again' as ghosts – that much of what is non-contemporary may still concern us? Ibsen may perhaps become more relevant precisely by liberating him from the clammy embrace of the obvious. Might we not even profit from daring to ask what it would take for *Ghosts* to become, once again, homeless?

Can we imagine a decanonisation of *Ghosts*, a way of reviving the strangeness and the radical aspects of this play that once plagued the censors and led to its being banned, that once made it seem so demoralising? The German literary critic, Hans Robert Jauss, suggests one possible way of doing so. What he does is challenge us to maintain a dual awareness that encompasses our own historical context, as well as the text's historical context. Might it not be somewhere in the trafficking between horizontal expectations of the past and the present that the most fruitful interpretations arise, thus avoiding both the naive insistence on 'relevance' and the rigidities of a purely historical experience of the play? For this to happen we need to seek out encounters with the strange as well as the apparently familiar aspects of the text.

It seems that a number of aspects of the plot of *Ghosts*, as well as its choice of theme and form, still have a potential relevance. The task of finding out which, and how, is that of every new reader of the text, which is now almost 125 years old. Perhaps the most enduring dimension of *Ghosts* is, ultimately, its thorough exploration of the past's influence on the present. To move on, it might be important to keep Captain Alving's memory alive.

– – –

Tore Rem (1967) is Professor of British Literature at the University of Oslo's Institute for Literature, Area studies and European languages. He is also a book reviewer for *Dagbladet*. He has published a number of articles and books, in both Norwegian and English , especially on English and Scandinavian literature in the 19th century. The history of the book is one of his special fields. Here his publications include the anthology *Bokhistorie (*Book history) (2003) and a study of Alexander Kielland's writings entitled *Forfatterens strategier* (Strategies of the author) (2002). Rem is currently working on an extensive study of the early reception of Ibsen in Great Britain.

UNNIVERSARY AND OBSTINACY

Afterword to *An Enemy of the People*
by Nikolaj Frobenius

Can we imagine something other than an Ibsen anniversary? For example, an unniversary? Would the great writer be better suited by that?

There is often something almost nauseating about the celebration of the kings and queens of art. Almost invariably, I am left with the feeling that the chief actor would have been irritated by the whole business, or regarded the celebration as a declaration that one's artistic activity is now null and void.

The centenary of Ibsen's death occurs in 2006 and with a few potentially challenging exceptions, it looks as though the celebrations will in the main be both pompous and iconographic. The portraits adorning the material sent out by the National Committee for the Promotion of Ibsen, or the cover of the book you are holding in your hands, show an Ibsen familiar to us from infant school to the culture section of the newspaper; elevated, stern, unapproachable. In the midst of an anti-hierarchical pop culture we can read the pictures as caricatures of an outmoded cultivation of the genius. And yet the pictures give the stubborn dramatist an authoritarian aura that cements him ever more firmly in a historical pose that makes him remote and inaccessible to us.

But there is another Ibsen.

An argumentative, provocative, stubborn and prickly sod.

The argumentative side of Ibsen is often overlooked in favour of more universal and existential readings. But the quarrelsome is central if we want to try to get to grips with Ibsen's dramatic texts. The stubborn old sod releases pure aggression into his texts and the Ibsenite rage is often directed at his own country. For that reason, there is something oddly paradoxical about a centenary that celebrates Ibsen as a national icon.

'I want to live in permanent opposition. That is why I write ...' said the Austrian writer Thomas Bernhard. For a writer like that, a spectacular celebration is a wake.

The glossy literature sent out by the aforementioned National Committee states, among other things, that Henrik Ibsen created the modern drama and that his writing is 'alive and relevant, constantly rejuvenating new generations in their attitude towards the world's drama'. Here some of the most common clichés about the dramatist are repeated: that he is 'always relevant' and that 'Ibsen's themes are almost more relevant today than they were a hundred years ago'. Ibsen himself once wrote that any truth is viable for an average of seventeen years, sometimes twenty. Ibsen would probably have regarded our tendency to reproduce the truths of his plays a hundred years on as a sign of serious ill-health in a democratic welfare state.

This ceaseless harping on about Ibsen's relevance is perhaps the greatest hindrance to focusing on the human and political dynamite in his plays. Ibsen's relevance, his importance for social debate and his radical humanism are no doubt a precondition for the way in which we think of ourselves as radical Norwegians. But when I read Ibsen, when I see Ibsen, when I think about Ibsen, it strikes me that Ibsen himself would have been uncomfortable with the unassailability he has acquired, and that the admiration is not far removed from the spineless flattery of the compact majority which he attacked so furiously in one of his most barbed plays, *An Enemy of the People*, from 1882.

Part of the strategy to turn Ibsen into a national icon has involved promoting the dramatist's benevolent humanism at the expense of the elitist misanthropy in his plays.

Ibsen's great ambivalence towards Norwegianness and to Norwegian culture is readily apparent in the dramatist's literary attitude. Henrik Ibsen's abuse of the 'Norwegian way' is something we savour with a self-contempt that is poorly disguised as well as masochistic. This sniggering 'self-revelation' has been one of the most potent tools in the concerted effort to turn Ibsen into a national icon here in Norway.

This is, of course, the well-known strategy of assimilation: to praise the critic is the best way to get him to shut up.

In case anyone has forgotten, *An Enemy of the People* is about Dr Tomas Stockmann and his struggle for the purity of his hometown – both physical and spiritual. Stockmann discovers that the local spa – his own life's work – has been polluted. To begin with he is hailed as a hero by the townspeople. But the mood in the town changes when the cost of dealing with the problem becomes clear: our hero finds himself opposed by the local press, as well as his own brother, the sheriff. At a public meeting he mounts a frontal assault on the compact majority, declaring that he would rather see the town of his birth destroyed than prosper on a lie.

Doctor Stockmann: Yes yes; you can shout me down; but you can't deny me. The majority has *power* – alas – but *right* it does not have. Right is what I have – along with a few others, the chosen. The minority is always right.

In the performances we have seen of the play, Dr Tomas Stockmann is usually placed in the centre of the radical-humanistic landscape as a real hero with a valuable message. A closer reading of the play, however, reveals that Ibsen's portrayal of Stockmann is a lot more subtle and problematic. Ibsen's text makes it quite clear that Stockmann is very vain in his idealism. The fanatical outburst of hatred for public opinion in the play's third act is usually underplayed, or else treated as the passing expression of an understandable frustration. It is rare for a production to allow Stockmann's misanthropy to overshadow his well-intentioned idealism. The elitist and aristocratic aspects of Stockmann's attitude are often played down until they seem merely the expression of his frustrated radicalism rather than a true reflection of his anger. It is usual to relate this aspect of the public meeting to an ambivalent overall understanding of Stockmann's character. But it is possible to read it as an unmasking and not an aberration. Stockmann bubbles over here, and we get to see another side of him. He loses control and in this moment of lost control, Ibsen shows his stubbornness and his sharp edge.

Hovstad: It almost seems as though the doctor's intention is to destroy the town.

And later:

Doctor Stockmann (with growing fury): It should be razed to the ground, I tell you! And wiped out, like vermin, all of those who live with the lie.

As *An Enemy of the People* opens, Stockmann is blissfully content to be a friend of the people. By the time it ends, however, he is ragingly, furiously concerned about being an enemy of the people. Stockmann is mollified to become at the least an enemy of the majority and this gradually becomes his obsession. He becomes enamoured of his own image as a public enemy. He feels a *negative pride* in being denounced as an enemy of the people and step by step distances himself from the philanthropy that he has earlier expressed.

As I read the play, Ibsen uses Stockmann to describe one possible outcome of the radical project. In the course of the public meeting he moves to a position that is frankly neurotic. One moment he is defending his stance in the debate over the water source, the next he is proposing the extermination of his own neighbours. Some of his dialogue might have easily come from the mouths of the extreme fundamentalists of our own time.

Doctor Stockmann: … let this whole land be laid waste, let this whole people be exterminated!

Instead of seeing Stockmann's speech at the public meeting as a temporary aberration of character, we can read it as a centrifugal point in the play. An exasperated rage around which the rest of the text orbits. In *Mao II*, Don DeLillo writes of the author as a person who sits in small, dark rooms and identifies himself with the destroyers of his times, the terrorists and assassins. DeLillo describes impotence in a world where the terrorists have taken over the anger of the writers. In a world reduced to diffusion and surplus, terrorism is the only meaningful activity left, says the spokesman for the terrorists, while the novelist, Bill Gray, tries to insist on literature's multiple and democratic voice.

In *An Enemy of the People*, the path from well-meaning critic to furious destroyer is already astonishing short. Is Ibsen saying something about the anger implicit in radicalism? An anger that the radical protects, that energises him in his isolation. But that also enables him to wish for the extinction of his hometown because it has rejected him. What do we see beneath Dr Stockmann's genial exterior? Embittered melancholy. Cold hatred of the others. The last post of the radical's anger is not an aristocratic, lonely position on a remote island outside society, but also the wish to annihilate all that once assembled the powers of goodness in a shining thought. The pendulum has swung. Only distaste remains. Distaste. Dislike. Barren rage. Exterminate every last one of the bastards.

The unmasking of this rage, that for me is what *An Enemy of the People* is about.

The whole crowd (shouting): Yes, yes, yes! He's an enemy of the people! He hates his own country! He hates everyone!

– – –

Nikolaj Frobenius was born in 1965. He has an M.A. in Film from the London Institute. Frobenius has written several novels, including *Latour's Catalogue* and most recently *Theory and Practise*. In addition to novels he has also written screenplays, including *Insomnia*. He has also been editor of the literary journal *Vinduet* (The Window), and is currently employed as feature film consultant at the Norwegian Film Fund. He is working on a new book.

PATIENCE, WILD DUCKS, VILLAINS AND HEROES

Afterword to *The Wild Duck* by Helene Uri

At times when I run dry of ideas, I turn to the Patience programmes on my computer. I love jigsaw puzzles. As students we dissected Ibsen's plays under the guidance of experts and that was when I first discovered all the Patience games and jigsaw puzzles in these dramas, how everything works out, how all the bits fit together. Ever since, this has been a central part of the pleasure I derive from Ibsen. And it is why I am so fond of crime mysteries. In other words, I like Ibsen for many of the same reasons that I also like Agatha Christie: that apparently superficial dialogue acquires a deeper meaning before we reach the end of the play. That goes for every last one of them.

The Wild Duck is a play with several themes, as all good literature should be. It is about the relationship between parents and children. It is, at least peripherally, about women's liberation. It is about truth and lies, power and wealth, poverty and social fall, the power of language. The play is realistic in the sense that the characters do not do impossible things such as fly about with propellers on their backs or live in a rubbish bin. This, of course, does not prevent it from being replete with symbols.

Wild ducks

I can't remember exactly when I read *The Wild Duck* for the first time. Maybe it was at secondary school, maybe later. But my grandfather read me Welhaven's poem about the wild duck quietly swimming and the hunter who shoots it, when I was a small child:

> A wild duck swims quietly
> Along the island's high coast;
> The clear waves play
> Around its pure breast.
>
> A hunter squats
> In the steep scree
> And for his sport shoots
> The lovely creature.
>
> And the bird cannot go
> To the sweet shelter of a nest
> And the bird will not complain
> Of its pain and its need.
>
> And so it quietly dives
> Down into the dark fjord,
> And the cold waves close over
> And wipe out its traces.

Grandfather. Grey trousers, white shirt, always a white shirt. "What does 'for his sport' mean, grandfather?" "It means 'for fun'" grandfather replied. I realised then that not only had the wild duck died and gone down into the dark waters forever, but that the hunter had done this for fun. There on my grandfather's lap I wept, my tears darkening his white shirt. Later, when reading or watching the play, I've found myself wondering whether this is true of wild ducks: if they are wounded, do they really dive down to the bottom and hold on? Having spoken to a professor at the Veterinary College, and another from the Institute of Biology at the University of Oslo, I can confirm that it is a myth. Okay.

Welhaven, and several of the characters in *The Wild Duck*, propagate the myth, as is their perfect right. But Ibsen – Ibsen himself – has Hedvig's wild duck dive down and hold on to the vegetation at the bottom, after having been winged by the short-sighted businessman, Werle, only to be brought back to the surface by Werle's clever dog. This, according to our ornithological experts, could not have happened. Yet Ibsen no doubt wants us to believe this part of the play. Writers carried out pretty poor background research in those days, eh? Take the zoological play away from your average reader, and... and what? The play collapses? No, it really doesn't matter all that much, does it? Because the image of the wild duck diving down in order to ensure its own death is so sad, so beautiful, and so apposite. While the most driven, fact-orientated souls can simply pretend to themselves that they are unaware of the zoological realities of the situation. In one sense, *The Wild Duck* consists entirely of wild ducks, staggering around after having been winged and – like the duck in the drying loft – living in a make-believe world: Gregers Werle with his desire to tell everyone the truth; old Ekdal who goes hunting among the withered Christmas trees and dusty rabbits; Gina, who has been seduced and rejected; Hjalmar Ekdal with his invention, not to mention the two drunkards living on the floor below. The super wild duck is, of course, Hedvig.

It doesn't matter if Hjalmar has more lines, Hedvig is the main character. In my mind she will always be associated with a black-and-white photograph of Anne Marit Jacobsen from a television production in 1970. A grainy and unclear image. Jacobsen's white, arched forehead. Is she wearing a checked frock and a ponytail? I don't know. It isn't important. My Hedvig does.

Hedvig is 14 years old, poised between childhood and adulthood. An exciting age. But to tell the truth, Hedvig has never really fascinated me, but rather irritated me. She's so hopelessly naive. Listening to Hedvig is like listening to the fairy tale about Butterball. Doesn't she realise what's going on? No, she's as stupid as Butterball. Here's that old witch banging on the door again – surely Butterball isn't going to creep down in the sack yet again? But oh yes, that's what he does. And Hedvig is like him. Just as naive, just as credulous. Some have maintained that Hedvig has the soul of an artist at an early stage of development. Well, I don't buy that. I prefer to think she's a little retarded (not that these are necessarily mutually exclusive – she could still be a young artist for all that). Either she was born like that, or she's become like that from living with an incorrigible father and an alcoholic grandfather, taken early from school as well. Retarded or not, she is every bit the impractical dreamer Hjalmar is, even though he probably isn't her real father. And besides being naive, Hedvig is kind. Patient and kind. She's kind to her father, her mother, her grandfather. Nothing but goodness and light, that's Hedvig. She never protests. In other words: not a typical teenager.

But the fascination with language, as when she questions the expression *the briny depths* (havsens bund), is something I share with her – and this is where she touches me. Hedvig notes, among other things, that when Gregers speaks it's "as though he meant something other than what he said all the time." The point is fatal, for when Gregers asks her to sacrifice the wild duck, Hedvig shoots herself instead.

Villains

It is the businessman who has winged Hedvig's duck. But isn't he actually the one who has winged all of them? "For his sport"? Without actually realising what it would lead to? Is the businessman, Werle, the villain of *The Wild Duck*? He is mean. Moreover he is rich. He has several crimes on his conscience: he works to establish a relationship with his housekeeper, Fru Sørby, so that she'll be able to look after him when he loses his sight completely. He has earlier tricked old Lieutenant Ekdal in a business partnership, so it was Ekdal who ended up in jail. According to his son, Gregers, he also drove his wife – Gregers' mother – to her death. Moreover, Werle seduced the maidservant Gina and probably got her pregnant before marrying her off to the simple, unsuspecting Hjalmar Ekdal, son of Lieutenant Ekdal. Hedvig is Gina's daughter and her father is in all probability the businessman – for she too is in the process of losing her sight.

Hjalmar Ekdal – Hedvig's hopeless father – calls himself a photographer; but everyone, except perhaps he himself, knows that it is his wife who does most of the work. Hjalmar does a bit of retouching now and then, and the work suits him perfectly: he prettifies the pictures and makes reality more beautiful. Had Hjalmar been born a hundred years later he would have been among the first to eat sushi and sashimi (though he would hardly have been able to afford them more than once in while). Hjalmar would have been up waving his bottle of balsamic vinegar when the rest of us were still stuck with the usual 5% vinegar. Hjalmar is pretentious, a real snob. He won't have it when his old childhood friend Gregers, who hasn't seen him for 17 years, says he's 'filled out a lot'. No, he's just become a little more 'manly'. Old Ekdal was a coward for not taking his own life after the scandal broke, Hjalmar declares, whereas he – Hjalmar – showed his courage in choosing to live. Hjalmar has really discovered the magical power of language: he turns himself into the man he wants to be. And it looks as though he has managed to fool others besides himself: Gregers Werle at any rate has remarkable faith in him and Hedvig is – naturally – naive enough to believe in him. But he does not fool us.

His self-centredness and his pretensions make Hjalmar almost evil. He refuses to recognise his own father as the old man passes through Werle's sumptuous rooms in his rags. Hjalmer's best quality is his love for his daughter, but even that isn't quite enough. When he comes home from the dinner party, he finds he has forgotten his promise to bring back something delicious for Hedvig and it isn't easy for him to understand that the menu he brings home doesn't taste quite as good to Hedvig as the food would have done. Even though Hedvig enjoys a bit of linguistic magic herself, she's sufficiently like her practical mother to find that imagining a few tasty mouthfuls is nowhere near as good as eating them would be. Hjalmar knows that Hedvig is not supposed to strain her eyes, but is so lazy that he allows her to do retouching work anyway, while he plays up in the loft. And it gets worse: Gregers goes for a walk with Hjalmar between the third and fourth acts and in the course of it Hjalmar learns that Gina has had an affair with the businessman. Later Fru Sørby tells him that she and the businessman are going to marry, so that she will be able to take care of him once he's lost his sight. When next the businessman arrives with a gift enclosed in a letter for Hedvig, Hjalmar puts two and two together, and for once it comes to four – at which he promptly and in the crudest possible fashion betrays Hedvig. We all know how it ends.

It is hinted that Hjalmar is the way he is as a result of being brought up by two aunts. It won't do lad – you're despicable!

And now that we mention it, we might as well ask how Gregers came to be like he is – a big-talking gossipmonger, a fanatic, a blind seeker of truth. We know his father, the businessman, and none of us would probably want him as a close friend or a partner in a firm. Greger's mother had problems with her nerves, although we don't quite know whether to believe the father or the son's version of what happened to her. And hang on a minute – maybe old Werle isn't so bad after all. If he's a sinner, he's at least a repenting sinner. He's looking after old Ekdal, he sends the gift in a letter to Hedvig, he makes an honest woman of Fru Sørby and he tries to bring about a reconciliation with Gregers. So maybe he isn't a villain after all? Maybe the old business-man is another of the wild ducks? He bemoans his loneliness and the onset of his blindness. His son rejects him. Isn't Gregers a much more villainous type than his father? We might try to excuse his be-haviour because of his difficult upbringing, but the train of events he sets in motion is both irreversible and unforgivable. He is responsi-ble for the death of an innocent child; no-one can bring Hedvig back to life again. I won't ever be able to forgive Gregers.

Heroes

Don't people need to be able to hide behind a life-lie or two? To shel-ter from harsh realities, to hold fast to a dream, an illusion, a fantasy? One fine day, not long from now, I'll win the football pools. Or may-be I'll get a contract with a record company. I'll be thin and beautiful. Rich and famous. Dr Relling advocates such an attitude. "Take the life-lie from the average person and you take away their happiness too", Relling announces, though he can hardly have foreseen that his words would become *The Wild Duck's* most famous quotation. Ac-cording to Relling, it can be dangerous to look reality straight in the eye. It is not necessarily healthy to be forced to concede that one will never be anything other than an average person handing in the football pools coupon, but never getting more than ten right, con-demned for the rest of your life to drive a second-hand station wagon made in Japan and not a limousine with your own chauffeur. That one doesn't have enough talent to get a record contract, or to make the Great Discovery. We know that in many ways the world is a ter-rible place, all we need to do is remind ourselves that here on our half of the planet we spend a fortune on slimming cures while those on the other side are starving to death. That's why we need somewhere like the loft, a place to play, to let the imagination roam free and forget about reality. Both Relling and I agree on that. Maybe Relling isn't exactly loveable, but we should remember that he doesn't reveal so much of his cynical ideas about the life-lie until he feels compelled to do so. He does so only to stop the insane Gregers, but once Relling has really got going then he does his utmost to deprive him of his life-lie. But Gregers, after all, deserves it. Dr Relling is not such a bad guy after all. He's a good psychologist, but hardly the stuff of which heroes are made?

Is it the case that a serious work of literature should have a hero? Or a heroine? I don't know. According to some, there are neither heroes nor heroines in *The Wild Duck*, only victims. But for me there is one heroine. Gina, Hedvig's mother, is the heroine of the play, with her swaying hips and her felt slippers. Today Gina would hardly have chosen felt slippers for her footwear. While Hjalmar waltzed around with his balsamic vinegar and his flute and wished he could afford the latest Nokia, Gina would be shuffling around in practical Ecco shoes and buying her clothes from Hennes and Mauritz. Gina can't afford designer clothes, but then again she doesn't want them, nor does she have time. Hjalmar, on the other hand, has his nose pressed up close to the shop window.

Gina is the wisest, even if she doesn't know how to use loan words properly. She is the pragmatist, evaluating situations and adapting to them. Greger's goal in life is to promote 'the claim of the ideal', Gina's is to keep the family together, even if that means baby-talking smug, fat, pompous Hjalmar, looking after his drunken father, keeping the books and even doing Hjalmar's job for him. But Gina is, above all else, a mother and for Hedvig's sake she goes on. It might be the case that a woman of Gina's class had few alternatives in those days; nevertheless, in my view it is the maternal obligation that decides Gina's fate for her. Gina is a noble, real and simple person. She is tolerant and incredibly generous. She never chides Hjalmar. She doesn't even blame Gregers for Hedvig's death. She claims to believe Gregers when he says he meant well. And when Hedvig's dead body is carried out of the loft, Gina says to Hjalmar that 'now at least, I know we share her', and I think she says it with no bitterness, no irony in her voice. And anyway, double-talking is not in Gina's nature. Ibsen gives his personae linguistic characteristics. Hjalmer loves his ornate expressions. He declares floridly that he has been 'struck by fate's punishing blow' to his head. Gina wreaks havoc with loan words. This is her linguistic trademark in the play. Its effect on stage is no doubt intended to be comic, to show that she comes from a different social background to the other characters. If Gina is as smart as I think she is, she would have had the correct pronunciations down pat – *if*, that is, it had seemed important. But it does not. No linguistic high-jinx for Gina. She has a wholly practical attitude towards language: its purpose is to enable communication. Gina has no time for vague talk of the loft as the 'the briny depths', and wild ducks that are actually something else, or fantasies about being a dog. And if Hjalmar understands what she means when she says 'pigstol', then why on earth should she stop saying it? It has been suggested that Gina uses these foreign words in an attempt to please her husband. I don't agree. That being so, I believe she would quickly have learned to use them correctly. I prefer to think of it as Gina's small protest against her dreadful husband's vanity that comes bubbling out here, a protest that she otherwise takes care to conceal. And when Gregers complains that the air in the home is stale, she responds that she has already aired it; when he says that the room seems dark and sad and she responds by removing the light shade, this is her way of protesting against this creepy windbag who threatens to destroy the home she has made for Hedvig.

The play is over, and we have left the theatre, our handkerchiefs wet, our eyes red, our hearts heavy. What happens afterwards? Could there be something between Gina and Dr Relling? Life has dealt them some heavy blows, but deep down they share the same healthy, cautious attitude. I think that once Gina has recovered she will see that there is no longer any point in being married to Hjalmar, now Hedvig is dead. We know Dr Relling has previously proposed to Fru Sørby and been rejected. Now he has become a dedicated drinker and an uncompromising cynic, but deep down inside he remains a profoundly good man. Once Gina has shuffled around him a bit and he has calmed down himself, I think the two could live out the rest of their lives together in some contentment. I hope they think so too, for that would lighten the ending considerably. And the two cards left at the end of a game of Patience would find their use in a better game.

– – –

Helene Uri has written novels, popular science, and non-fiction books for children, young adults, and adults. Her books have been translated into many languages. Her background is in language studies and she has a Master's degree in the Scandinavian languages and a doctorate in linguistics. She was for many years employed at the University of Oslo but is now a full-time writer.

GUILT

Afterword to *Rosmersholm* by Finn Skårderud

We feel guilt. There's no avoiding guilt. That's good, and it's not so good.

Rosmersholm can help us gain a better understanding of this. This is an advanced and demanding theatrical text which can be read as Henrik Ibsen's major examination of the *sensation of guilt* and not least, the relationship of this feeling to the dream of creating greater freedom for people. 'Liberation' is a word he uses frequently. This play is from 1886. Seven years previously, Ibsen liberated Nora in *A Doll's House*. By the time of *Rosmersholm*, he knew perhaps a little more. Here he shows us that freedom is actually a pretty complicated business. And guilt is part of what complicates it.

Rosmersholm is a study in double decline. The old, with its stupefying guilt, is on the way out. Guilt makes an invalid of the will. And if one destroys others, then the feeling of guilt itself can bring about one's own destruction. But the new is in decline too. To have freedom from guilt as a goal is perhaps both too greedy and too naive.

The Rosmersholm home is packed to the rafters with guilt. Guilt is a complex feeling. Sometimes it is based on external realities, on misdeeds and bad actions. At other times it is more diffuse and divorced from specific acts. There is not just one guilt, but many, and these overlap and merge with each other. And they overlap into other emotional states, such as shame, or depression. And rage. *Rosmersholm* is a play about nothing less than a triple murder. At the final curtain, the family line has been wiped out. It is all almost a bit too much.

Rosmersholm makes itself accessible to us here and now. Today it would not perhaps be as natural for us to use a word like 'freedom'. It is redolent of the past and of political and moral revolt. In our self-centredness, it is perhaps more likely that we would call it 'self-realisation'. And with that the play acquires a troublingly contemporary resonance. What is enough self-realisation? What is too much, what too little? How does this relate to guilt today – or shame? At what point does the pursuit of freedom from guilt become shameless?

More on this later.

Let us examine the manifold varieties of guilt in *Rosmersholm*. A natural starting point is what we might call *cultivated guilt*. It is already present in the first set of stage directions: 'Round about on the walls hang older and more recent portraits of priests, officers and government officials in uniform'.

Here are the representatives of faith, morality and ambition. They decide between right and wrong and where guilt and shame are appropriate reactions. Sigmund Freud related the guilt-inducing aspect of a culture to a specific psychological construct, the *superego*. That is the conscience. The norms are instilled in the child and in this way we monitor, judge and punish ourselves. We acquire our own internalised secret police. A strict upbringing can also induce a guilt that is *not* connected to our deeds.

The feeling of guilt can develop into an exaggerated state of self-criticism. We note its presence well, yet it hampers and limits us. A guilt like this can arise from a thought, a fantasy or a sexual desire. It is the stuff of which neuroses are made.

Guilt, along with shame, pride and embarrassment, is part of the complex feelings of self-consciousness. Other reactions, such as desire or anger, can arise more spontaneously, while the self-conscious feelings are connected to the evaluation of oneself in relation to others and to norms and ideals. Guilt and shame are feelings of self-evaluation that conclude that one has made a mistake. They quickly quash joy.

Most of Ibsen's dramas of contemporary life take some such established environment as their point of departure. There is something to be defended here, whether it be a position or a tradition. And it is threatened. In *Rosmersholm,* new ideas are making headway. They propose moral and social norms different to those which have governed middle-class behaviour for a long time. A revolution of the mind is prophesied. Parallel with Ibsen, Nietzsche published his ideas on freeing minds from religious faith and the burdens of morality and conscience. There are hardly grounds for claiming that the philosopher directly inspired the dramatist, or vice-versa, but they – like Freud – lived through the same era of modernisation, secularisation and the desire for the psychological liberation of the individual.

Nietzsche described the new man as 'a superman'; psychoanalysis was a therapeutic undertaking aimed at ameliorating cultural discomfort in the form of neurotic guilt, while the dream at Rosmersholm is of creating 'happy and noble people'. A happy nobility such as this is first and foremost associated with the dream of 'the quiet, contented, safe feeling of freedom from guilt'. *Rosmersholm* shows us the ambivalent Ibsen. Himself someone who wished to bring about liberation from the cowing of guilt, he is also concerned here with showing the problems of such liberation.

Rebekka West has arrived from Finnmark, bringing with her these Nietzschean and atheistic ideals. And she introduces 'fresh birch twigs and wild flowers' into the rooms. The dead wife, 'poor Beate', was not able to tolerate these, being confused by both the scents and the colours. Pastor Rosmer indulges his enthusiasm for the new atmosphere of vitality in the old country home. He becomes a Christian apostate. This can be interpreted as a settling of accounts with his father, as a declaration of his independence from the law and as a revolt against the portraits on the walls. But Rosmer's problem is that he has grown up in these rooms. Does he possess the spiritual energy for a reckoning of these dimensions?

Rosmer is an anti-hero. The text opens with Madam Helseth and Rebekka standing at the window and watching him up by the millrace. In the ensuing dialogue we learn that he is a wounded man. Something dramatic has taken place. There has already been one suicide. And we are introduced to some of his character traits. He is a man who does not dare. He takes the long way round to avoid unpleasantness.

He has been an indecisive man who has lived a passive life. His fear of the physical is such that one supposes him to suffer from both sexual anxiety and impotence. Any director of the play who decides to portray Rosmer as both boring and irresolute has Ibsen's authority to do so. But he is also a sensitive soul and we empathise with him. He is a dreamer, but he wants what is good. He wants to be a part of the more open and happy future. Rebekka has understood that he is the type of person who allows himself to be seduced. So she seduces him with promises of a more genuine life. But can he stand by his own new understanding of life? He does not have the mental resources and gives up with a worrying ease. Weakness and cowardice are and remain his hallmarks and these are not the marks of nobility.

Let us look at this in the context of guilt. Many have seen Rosmer's development through the play as a progress from weakness to strength, while Rebekka's is a movement in the opposite direction, from strength to weakness. Maybe so. Rosmer was a man unable to act, crippled by the scruples of his generation and he becomes a man of action who drives Rebekka and himself to suicide. Is that strength?

No. It is merely more of the same, plain and simple. The revelations entail an increase in guilt. The demonic power he shows in the final scene represents the final triumph of his guilt. Rosmer becomes a desperate man. He remains the same coward as before, going the long way round to avoid facing challenges. Instead of experiencing and growing, he chooses to destroy. We observe his primitive rage and he becomes a dangerous and reckless man. He seeks out power, looking to subvert his own impotence. On account of his guilt, he demands that Rebekka take her own life. And she, crushed as she is by her own guilt, makes a willing victim.

The concluding scene itself is left open. Daniel Haakonsen, an Ibsen expert, wrote in *Henrik Ibsen. The Man and the Artist*, that 'in this play Ibsen describes the full-blown myth of love – the myth of complete union between two people'. Again – maybe so. Is it a perfect union in love that sees the two of them end in the mill-race, along the lines of Romeo and Juliet? Is this atonement? Is this elevation to a higher plane? Is it not rather their final and most complete act of self-deception?

Fredrik Engelstad writes in *Love's labyrinths. Mind and Society in Ibsen and Bjørnson's Writings* that *Rosmersholm* cannot be read according to the traditional formulas of tragedy, as Haakonsen does. In classical tragedy there is a movement towards a purification and the deaths of the heroes illustrate their greatness. Ibsen's is a thoroughly modern perspective, writes Engelstad, and the play must be read as a psychological drama in which the writer's purpose is to 'bore down into the depths of the mind' in order to understand more.

Exactly. There is no purification for Rosmer and Rebekka, no greatness in them, and strictly speaking only meagre insight. A fall, in tragedy, should also imply an ascent. Here there is only falling. They descend into something raw and primitive. The conclusion is a brisk amputation. Veins and arteries are – literally – opened. There is bleeding. Those who find the ending problematic do so because it cannot end here. And our job then is to understand in order to go on understanding.

Sex is guilt. *Rosmersholm* is written within other parameters of embarrassment. Rebekka's guilt has multiple causes. When she confesses, she lays particular emphasis on her sexual desire for Rosmer.

REBEKKA: Then it came over me, – that wild, irresistible lust – Oh Rosmer! (…) It came over me like a storm over the sea. It was like one of those storms we get up there in the north. It takes you, and whips you along with it, as far as it pleases. No chance of resisting.

Rebekka describes her own development in three stages: Will – Lust – Love. Her great anxiety about the subject of her own sexuality is again a reminder of the importance of cultural taboos in the formation of guilt. Rebekka nevertheless resists her own desire and discovers that in the place of lust, her love for Rosmer is growing. But a love like this is devoid of joy. She has been tamed. 'The Rosmerian attitude to life is ennobling – but you know, it kills off happiness as well'.

Today we look somewhat differently upon our sexual desires.

And then there is of course the case of *justified guilt*. Rebekka comes to Rosmersholm with her philosophy of freedom and her vitality. But ambition grew in her too, and a selfish devilment. She wanted to be mistress of Rosmersholm and began to spin her web of intrigue. This was based on guilt too. The aim was to burden Beate with so much guilt that she would step aside. Rebekka played on her child-lessness. The childless Beate drowned herself in the falls, so that Re-bekka might give birth to a legitimate heir to the estate and carry on the line.

Rosmer's contribution to the spiritual murder of Beate is not so much what he does but what he doesn't do. The sin of omission is also a kind of action. Rosmer's betrayal lies in the fact that he neither saw nor understood Beate. In despair over her childlessness she has offered herself. It frightened him:

ROSMER: I told you about her uncontrollable, wild passion – which she wanted me to reciprocate. Oh, what fear she inspired in me!

Beate is spoken of as though she were mentally unbalanced. But we begin to suspect, not least from the minor characters, that she was perhaps not so much unbalanced as in deepest despair. Part of Ros-mer's blindness lies in his inability to distinguish between passion and madness, or to see that her state of mind might be the result of his rejection of her.

Let us introduce yet another possible source of guilt. Referring to its inventor, we might call it *Freudian guilt*. Its reality is debatable, both in general and in the context of this play in particular. For some, *Rosmersholm* is a play of particular interest because Sigmund Freud wrote about it.

In Freud's collected works we find a total of six references to Hen-rik Ibsen. Five are merely passing references, of which one is a ref-erence to the writer and four to the plays (*The Wild Duck, A Doll's House, Little Eyolf,* and *An Enemy of the People).* The sixth and most extensive is his analysis of *Rosmersholm,* eight pages long, originally published in the psychoanalytic magazine, *Imago,* in 1916 and trans-lated into English in 1925. In the official, twenty-four volume English language version of the collected works, *The Standard Edition of the Complete Psychological Works of Sigmund Freud,* the text is one of three essays published as *Some Character-types Met With in Psycho-analytic Work.* The study of *Rosmersholm* is part of the second essay, *Those Wrecked by Success.* Here Rebekka West is joined by Lady Macbeth. According to the title, it appears that these two women lose as a result of having won.

The key scene in the play is the one in which Rebekka finally achieves her goal and Rosmer offers her marriage for the first time. To begin with there is enthusiastic acceptance and 'cries of joy'. But then she rejects him. Why? According to Freud, it is because the *unconscious* enters the arena. Guilt stops her short. It is a matter, says Freud, not only of the justified sense of guilt she feels, but also of an unconscious guilt related to something in her past. At this point in the play, the detective-like Rector Kroll (Beate's brother) has not yet acquainted Rebekka with his speculation that she is the biological daughter of Dr West. But Freud proposes that she unconsciously knows this and that as the lover of the doctor, she 'knows' she has been living in an incestuous relationship. For this reason she is unable to accept Rosmer's offer.

Oedipus comes to Rosmersholm. Freud was an outstanding man of letters. Part of his story-telling talent lay in the way he was able to connect his clinical experiences to familiar myths and solid metaphors. Freud's great story is the *Oedipus complex*. He turned Sophocles' tragedy about King Oedipus into the central myth of psychoanalysis. Oedipus tore out his own eyes after gaining insight into the fact that he had killed his father and lain with his mother. He 'tore out' the insight. On this mythological basis, Freud maintained the universality of the notion that children have fantasies about loving their parent of the opposite sex and becoming the rival of the other. A triangle like this, according to the Viennese doctor, is a fundamental condition of, and almost the primal mover of our spiritual lives.

So Freud proposes the Rosmer – Beate – Rebekka triangle as a repetition of the Dr West – mother – Rebekka triangle. And it is this guilt-complex that overwhelms Rebekka at the moment of proposal, when she realises that she will be replacing Beate, just as she once replaced her mother. At this point it is wise to remember that the Oedipus complex is far from being a scientific truth – as well as also being a monumental diversion here.

Nor is there in the play any authority for claiming that an incestuous relationship is involved. If Freud reads this into the text, it is perhaps not only because he is wearing his own theoretical glasses as he writes, but also because Ibsen laid some elegant literary bait. There are probably many of us who, without having been influenced by Freud, sense the presence of incest. We are readers/ audience and we *co-write* as fact that the relationship between Dr West and Rebekka was a sexual reality. Once again we bow to the writer's skill in constructing emotional realities. In his notes to *Rosmersholm*, Ibsen was actually more explicit about the incestuous nature of the relationship.

To return to the key scene. Once more it is Fredrik Engelstad, in the book mentioned earlier, who helps us to glimpse new possibilities. Rosmer asks for Rebekka's hand in marriage. He needs Rebekka as his wife in order to rid himself of the burden of guilt associated with Beate. He cannot go through life with a corpse on his back. But what sort of proposal is that? He wants to use Rebekka as a tool in his own spiritual housekeeping. He is perhaps not the kind of husband she has been dreaming of, nor is this the state of freedom from guilt of which she has been dreaming. Rosmer's proposal does not come from a spiritual aristocrat, it comes rather from a spiritual slave. He is begging.

So now Narcissus too has arrived at Rosmersholm. In his relationship to both Beate and Rebekka, it is striking how little of their reality Rosmer is able to ingest and the extent to which he is in orbit around himself. In his despairing grief over Beate, Rosmer becomes so preoccupied with his own guilt that he loses sight of Rebekka, and becomes guilty of the same crime against her. Yet more of the same. He sees himself and not others and he does not see what he is doing.

Based on the second of psychoanalysis' two central myths, we might call this Rosmer's *narcissism*. The source is Ovid's *Metamorphoses*. The myth is about Narcissus, who died by a small lake while staring at his own reflection in the water. One interpretation is that he loved himself too well. Another is that he did not love himself enough. He who has too little, needs more – and takes more. Narcissism can be defined as a state of psychological immaturity in which greatness and littleness, impotence and omnipotence live side by side in disharmony, and in which an insecure sense of self is the essence. Rosmer has his grandiose fantasies about how he alone will unite and ennoble all people. At the same time he gathers to himself what he thinks he needs, nourished by his own littleness. The leap into the falls can be understood as both the aggressive and the despairing expression of this kind of immaturity.

Ibsen's examination of the problems involved here is valuable. In our culture of self-realisation we often read and hear statements to the effect that we ought to exclude guilt and shame from our lives. Let us fervently hope that this never happens. It will entail a brutalisation. A shameless realisation of the self might well involve crude offence to others, trampling on them, an inability to see their needs. And someone who is not able to feel or to deny guilt is a close relative of the type popularly known as the psychopath.

Guilt and shame are social feelings, necessary in order to protect others and to keep our own grandiose thoughts in check. In our everyday lives and in psychiatry, when we speak of guilt and shame as problematic, it is because there can be too much of them. That which should protect becomes, instead, self-destructive. What we then have is a dosage problem.

We can read Ibsen's psychodrama as a reminder that there is no freedom without responsibility, nor any self realisation without compassion for others. The aggressive form of self-realisation has a sad tendency to end in loneliness.

– – –

Finn Skårderud (b.1956) is a psychiatrist, author and professor. He is an internationally renowned expert in the field of eating disorders. He has his own psychotherapeutic practice in Oslo, as well as working for the Norwegian Olympic Committee as a psychiatrist for leading athletes. He is attached to the High School in Lillehammer as Professor of Health and Social Studies. His most recent books are a play entitled *Quisling. Undersøkelsen* (Quisling. The Examination) (2005) (with Øystein Lønn); *Andre reiser* (Other Journeys) (2004); *Sterk/svak. Håndboken om spiseforstyrrelser.* (Strong/weak. The handbook of eating disorders) (2000), *Federico Fellini* (1999) and *Uro. En reise i det moderne selvet* (Disquiet. A journey into the modern self) (1998).

FREE-WILL WIFE

Afterword to *The Lady from the Sea*
by Shabana Rehman

It is almost embarrassing to admit it: I never feel more Pakistani than when I read an Ibsen play. *The Lady from the Sea* is a drama that it is wholly impossible for me not to relocate to another culture – in my case, the Pakistani.

But first a few words about the play's parameters. In *The Lady from the Sea* we meet Wangel, a country doctor, and his second wife, Ellida Wangel, who is stepmother to Hilde and Bolette, the daughters of Dr Wangel's first marriage. The daughters' mother died, after which Dr Wangel proposed to Ellida. She accepted and entered into a sort of marriage of convenience with him.

Ellida, and also Hilde and Bolette, are in many ways disenfranchised women in their age. They long to live independent and free lives and to avoid a relationship of dependence on men as their protectors. Can they permit themselves to have such dreams, at a time when men's attitude towards women, as well as women's upbringing, does not seem to offer anything else?

All three women are going through different stages of this process. Ellida Wangel struggles and longs for the freedom of an earlier time, before she sold herself in marriage, a time symbolically related to the sea and its mysterious power. Nor does the slightly younger stepdaughter, Bolette, want to be merely 'someone's wife'. She too, in the face of mild despair, carries on her struggle in the hope of becoming an independent person.

The Lady from the Sea is in many ways a psycho-romantic thriller. The play circles round the theme of arranged marriage, an arrangement in which both parties live as strangers to each other. Ellida, with her morning and evening swims, is almost neurotically obsessed by the sea, while Dr Wangel celebrates his dead wife's birthday in secret with his daughters.

Yet there are also beautiful things in the play. To my mind the most beautiful is that, whereas people in modern times make use of words and phrases like 'moody', 'low blood-sugar', 'alienation' and even PMS, Ibsen prefers to show us a female universe of oceans, of mystery and longing and of the individual's struggle for the right to choose. Ellida Wangel isn't happy in her role as 'landlubber', even though she accepted Dr Wangel's proposal of marriage. She does not dare to admit that she is out of touch with what lives inside her, until she is confronted with her past – the sudden reappearance of a former lover. Only then does she begin to admit the presence of the ocean storms and the resistance in her mind, and that it is her own responsibility to take action. She feels an erotic attraction towards the past and the sea, an attraction she is unable to shake off while she still feels the lack of choice in her life.

The Lady from the Sea can easily be transposed to our own time, a time in which it becomes increasingly evident that people are being denied the right to govern their own lives. There are people living with marital partners not of their own choosing and we find them everywhere, from upper-class white families to immigrant families, their minds constrained by the forces of religion, or by culture, or by financial considerations.

Love stories employing an East-West setting often describe the dissolution of the arranged marriage and the way in which both parties subsequently choose love. *The Lady from the Sea* shows us something quite different. Here Ellida Wangel achieves her own freedom only once she realises that she does not *have* to choose love, when she recognises her own responsibility at a quite different level. She realises that freedom of choice can mean something very different from the unpredictable hormonal explosion which free love seems to offer. This is the strongest and most readily accessible text I have yet come across about the struggle we humans wage against our fates each and every day.

What is it that turns a person into a victim? And what is it that means our choices can be called free?

Ibsen gives us several answers. As does life itself. Nothing is black and white.

The play is about the journey every person must take in order to become an actor – and not just a spectator – in the drama of his or her own life. For it is above all freedom of choice that forces us to realise, acknowledge and choose our course of action deliberately. It opens our eyes to what deep down is most important for us – that which in the last analysis make us alive. And so the play is also about something else: how can we set others free, at the same time as respecting our own free will?

But *The Lady from the Sea* goes one step further. The play does not conclude with the cliché that love always wins. In Ibsen's version, love has become a destructive erotic power which is simultaneously murderous, loyal and alluring. Ellida Wangel is deeply marked by her past, by the seaman to whom she was engaged, the one who disappeared, only to reappear again after she got married.

I know of several Pakistani girls who have found themselves in this dilemma. A typical end to such a story is that the girl finally agrees to marry the person chosen by her family – instead of the love of her youth. Even though her feelings for him are still powerful. He might be an ever so slightly 'criminal- second- generation' type of boy, someone with whom she has, in Bollywood fashion, exchanged rings, even though the family does not consider him good enough.

As for him, his reaction might be a restlessness, a tendency to infidelity and a hunger to be loved. He refuses to let go of his first love and yet he does not struggle hard enough to hold onto her.

Finally he disappears. Time passes. The family presently makes an offer that the girl – sadder but wiser, and ashamed of her own wildness – eventually agrees to accept. Within this marriage she can live a completely alienated life, with memories of her lover as the only elixir of life, and grow ill with shame. And she drifts towards a darkness where she can neither say yes to the life she is living – nor go back to her first love.

She was not allowed to choose herself. Life chose for her.

She did not leave the love of her youth, it was circumstances that took him from her. It was not she herself who chose to be the second wife of a man who already had children, and who could offer her economic security. Others did the choosing for her, because *they* thought it was best for her.

Oh yes, Ibsen's play has plenty of relevance to contemporary life. It can operate as a beacon for Muslim families in which it has almost become the fashion to rebel against arranged marriages. The play also has something to say about the traffic in human beings from Eastern Europe, people who are made victims, people for whom freedom of choice does not exist. Not to mention the postal order brides who continue to arrive in Norway each year, be they Russian or Thai.

One thing they all have in common is that they are all ladies from the sea.

In *The Lady from the Sea*, love is depicted as an illusion, as all love is doomed to be. Real love is linked to freedom of choice. When both external and internal realities allow people to choose freely, then they are liberated from their angst.

Ibsen brilliantly conveys this psycho-mystical aspect, which shows so clearly that a marriage is also an arena for the dramatic play of the psyche.

The Lady from the Sea can very readily be transposed to modern family life in Grønland in Oslo. The same issues are involved: you have your freedom to choose – what do you choose? The superficial love, or the common-sense marriage? Dare you choose that which you looked upon as compulsion? Do you dare to free yourself?

It takes courage to take responsibility for one's choices. The transformation in Ellida Wangel shows us this clearly. These are pressingly relevant dilemmas for thousands of ladies from the sea far removed from the realities of Norway today.

And yet we find them here in Norway too.

– – –

Shabana Rehman is operative in a number of arenas as writer, standup comedian and lecturer, always trying to break down taboos and encourage a greater openness. She has received a number of prizes for this. Rehman was born in Karachi and grew up in Oslo. She made her debut as a columnist in VG in 1996, and has completed studies in life-views, ethics and Scandinavian Studies. She has edited a multi-ethnic debating forum and given a number of lectures on the subject of equal rights for women, feminism and humour. See also www.shabana.no

HEDDA GABLER IN HOLLYWOOD

Afterword to *Hedda Gabler* by Audun Engelstad

"Had Shakespeare lived today, he would have been writing and producing films in Hollywood." This is a claim that is frequently repeated and in view of the fact that over the last decade his is one of the names that have appeared most frequently on the screen credits, the claim seems reasonable enough. But what about Ibsen, perhaps the most important dramatist of modern times? What sort of relationship would he have had to Hollywood? What is beyond dispute is that Hollywood has shown strikingly little interest in his plays, in spite of the fact that the theatre has played a crucial role in the development of film.

It has been claimed that Ibsen's use of form shows many similarities with the form of the feature film familiar to us today. Both the Ibsenite drama and the narrative of the classical realistic film try to give the public the illusion that what they are experiencing is a slice of real life, with ordinary people caught up in recognisable situations, speaking in the ways that people normally speak. Ibsen developed the use of an overtly relaxed dialogue which can also be used to express major insights and to carry dramatic situations. One also finds in Ibsen poisonous family situations with roots far back in the past, business ventures where failure has repercussions for the family's social life, and well-known character types. All of these are elements familiar from the majority of melodramatic films and television series.

Ibsen's plays have indeed been filmed a number of times and in a number of countries, but many of these have been filmed for television and in formal terms television drama is closer to the theatre than cinema. As for American film versions of Ibsen's plays, most of these stem from the era of the silent film, something which might seem paradoxical – it is, after all, what the characters say to each other that usually strikes us as being the essential aspect of Ibsen's plays – so the interest shown in them by these silent film producers suggests that the themes of his plays were regarded as popular.

Given, then, that Ibsen and Hollywood have so much in common, why have his plays not been more frequently turned into films, after the end of the silent era? On the surface it would seem as though his plays had all the ingredients necessary to attract screen adaptation after screen adaptation. With the introduction of the talkies at the end of the 1920s, there was an almost insatiable demand for stories with dialogue and a number of silent films were remade in talking versions. Hollywood studios had their own script departments and recruited their scriptwriters from among the ranks of novelists, journalists and playwrights. Among others, Arthur Miller and Tennessee Williams enjoyed great prestige in Hollywood and both counted Ibsen among their literary masters.

Add to this the fact that in the 1940s and 50s American contemporary culture – including Hollywood – was familiar with Sigmund Freud and psychoanalysis, and that psychoanalytic models of explanation were much used in these decades as an element of meaning in all types of film, from lavish main picture productions to genre-type B films, and the mystery deepens, as the distance between Freud and Ibsen is not great.

So it does seem something of a mystery that Ibsen's plays ceased to be the subject of film adaptations after 1930. Why were none of his modern plays used as the basis for major productions in the 1940s and 1950s, when the circumstances seemed so favourably inclined for such a development? Take *Hedda Gabler*, which has as its main character a fascinating *femme fatale*. For a long time, from the era of the silent film up to the 1930s, 40s and 50s, Hollywood could not get enough of such characters.

Historically, one can trace the roots of the *femme fatale* back to the plays, poems and visual art of the 19th century. Edvard Munch's 'Vampire' (1893) is one of the most frequently reproduced examples.

The chief characteristics of a *femme fatale* are her great strength of will and her calculation in pursuit of her own ends. She is dominating, provocatively direct and she does not hesitate to make use of her sexuality. As Munch's painting so clearly shows, involvement with her is dangerous and possibly fatal. *Hedda Gabler* lends itself readily to comparison with such artistic creations and the play was almost contemporary with Munch's painting. Though Ibsen does endow Hedda with a vulnerable side that the audience occasionally catches a glimpse of, her general behaviour throughout the play bears all the hallmarks of the *femme fatale*.

Marlene Dietrich is often mentioned among the most outstanding early examples of the type in the era of the talkie, with particular reference to Josef von Sternberg's *Der blaue Engel* (1930) and *Blonde Venus* (1932). But it was in the so-called *film noir* that the *femme fatale* character was most fully exploited. In the classic period of the *film noir*, from the mid-1940s to the mid-1950s, the *femme fatale* was an almost essential ingredient, either playing opposite the detective or as partner in crime or as a moving force behind men who willingly allowed themselves to be tempted into the criminal life.

It is not difficult to point to those places in the play where Hedda's 'fatal' side emerges. The first, symbolically enough, comes at the beginning of the second act, where Hedda fires off one of her pistols in an act of pure boredom. Playing with the technology of death like this becomes a way of making life bearable. This outwardly-directed death wish is a central aspect in the presentation of the *femme fatale* character. Critics of the classic *film noir* viewed the fatal woman as cynical and unscrupulous, devoid of the normal range of human emotions. It would not be right to describe Hedda thus, but in some situations she certainly approaches it. Recall, for example, how in the First Act she gains Thea's confidence the moment she realises that Thea has a close relationship to Løvborg, or how cunningly she tempts Løvborg to go out on the town at the end of the Second Act. These could be scenes from a *film noir* with Joan Bennett, Ava Gardner or Barbra Stanwyck playing the main role.

"For just once in my life, I want to have power over a human being's fate," says Hedda as an explanation for why she has done all this to Løvborg. This extends even to the point of deciding exactly what

kind of fate the person she has acquired power over should have. So
it is in accordance with the logic of the drama when Hedda, in the
final scene of the Third Act, gives Løvborg the pistol she has until
now been using to quell her intense boredom. Instead of telling the
distraught Løvborg that his manuscript will turn up again in a day
or two, she manipulates the conversation to the point where death
seems the only viable way out. As a coup de grace she even equips
him with the weapon that she aimed at him once before, just in case
he should suddenly rediscover the will to live ("– that was not my
worst cowardice – that afternoon"). In this way Hedda attaches her
fate to Løvborg's. The death wish is directed both inwards and outwards and the other pistol, which is still in the gun-case, will in the
end deal out the twinned fates.

Numerous articles on the *femme fatale* show that her fate is either
to be tamed by some tough guy – in other words, she bows to the
prevailing social norms of the patriarchy – or she dies. Hedda is not
the kind of woman who will allow herself to be tamed. She meets
her match in Judge Brack. The scene between the two of them in the
Fourth Act is, once again, like something taken from a *film noir*, with
an Edward G. Robinson or a Kirk Douglas in the role of Brack. Brack
reveals here an intimate knowledge of methods of police procedure,
as well as showing how to manipulate and trick the police authori-
ties. Services such as these do not, of course, come free – and here
Brack shows himself to be as hard-boiled as any underworld villain
from a *film noir*. Hedda's longing for complete power over another
finds its negative reflection in her own subjection to Brack, for now
it is her fate that is in the hands of another. Just as this subjection
proves fatal for Løvborg, so it gives the decisive final push to Hedda's
own death wish that eventually leads to her suicide.

There is clearly no lack of filmatic scenes in this play. The image
of Hedda shooting out of the back door in the low September sun is
dramatic in itself. And when Hedda opens the door of the woodstove
to burn the manuscript, we get an expressionist arrangement of light
with harsh side lighting in a close-up that accentuates the hardness
in her face and leaves the rest in shadow. The punch-drinking scene
in the Second Act, in which Brack and Tesman remain in the back
room, which has a glass door giving onto the room where Hedda and
Løvborg sit, would film very well in deep focus. And the exchange of

dialogue between Hedda and Brack is of a quick and sharp type that was long cultivated in Hollywood. But in spite of all these filmatic qualities, the familiar character types and the melodramatic themes, it is by no means certain *Hedda Gabler* could have been a successful Hollywood film.

Let's try a thought experiment: in 1951 Warner Brothers enjoyed great success with a filmed version of Tennessee Williams' play, *A Streetcar Named Desire*, directed by Elia Kazan, with Marlon Brando and Vivien Leigh playing the leads. The film won five Oscars and was nominated for another eight. One year previously, Jerry Wald had produced *The Glass Menagerie* for Fox without achieving the same kind of success, despite high expectations. These are historical facts. Suppose now that Wald tried to emulate the success of *A Streetcar Named Desire*, this time basing his film on a classic written by Williams' literary idol, Henrik Ibsen. What would be more natural than *Hedda Gabler*? Hedda is played by Barbra Stanwyck, Kirk Douglas is Brack, and Glenn Ford is cast as Løvborg. William Holden is to play Tesman, with Ida Lupino as Thea Elvsted and Lillian Gish as Aunt Julle. Michael Curtiz will direct the film, Budd Schulberg write the script, and John Alton is the executive producer. This is to be a melodrama with a strong element of *film noir*.

But what happens? Suppose now a screening of the film in Fox's studio, with Jerry Wald, Michael Curtiz and Budd Schulberg in attendance. As the scenes are played out across the screen, Wald puffs away on a cigar, slowly chewing it to bits. It's all here – the dramatic lighting, the coruscating exchange of dialogue, acting of the highest, Oscar-winning quality. When Hedda gives Løvborg the pistol, it's as though they both clasp it tightly a moment as Barbra Stanwyck gazes deeply into Glenn Ford's tormented, sweating face. Løvborg leaves and Hedda opens the stove and holds the manuscript as though it were a little child. The low camera angle makes Barbra Stanwyck's face look almost grotesque as the flames lick upwards. Jerry Wald wriggles uncomfortably in his chair and makes some notes. Cut to the next scene, as Aunt Julle arrives to announce that Aunt Rina is dead. Presently Tesman arrives and is told about the manuscript. Wald clears his throat and takes more notes. Then Brack arrives and describes what has happened to Løvborg. Despite the sparks flying between Barbra Stanwyck and Kirk Douglas, Wald seems completely uninterested. He has stopped taking notes and keeps looking up at the clock. And when Hedda shoots herself, he merely shakes his head and stubs out what's left of his cigar in the ashtray. All this despite the fact that John Alton's creative use of tracking shots and panoramas has managed to capture the interplay between what is going on in the sitting room and the backroom where Hedda is. The house lights go up and in the ensuing silence Jerry Wald lights, with exquisite care, a fresh cigar. Then he looks at Curtiz and says that the film needs first aid. After that he tells Schulberg that a few new scenes are needed, as well as some re-writing.

Is it really necessary to rewrite one of Ibsen's most powerful plays? What difficulties did this film adaptation encounter? The first is perhaps a minor one, at least, with regard to transferring a play to the screen, and is of a cultural nature. Jerry Wald would probably point out that all the references to children must be rewritten. The Hays office, which was the film industry's self-appointed censor, would hardly pass the scene where Hedda says she is burning Thea and Løvborg's child. It would be more suitable if she were to say 'now I am burning your life's work'. And all references to Hedda being pregnant would have to go if she is to end up committing suicide. And is it actually necessary that she take her own life? Løvborg, after all, was largely the author of his own misfortunes, unless it was in fact Diana who shot him. Might it not be morally more acceptable if Hedda is wounded by a stray shot and then sent to a hospital? And if she really must die, then at the very least her death must be presented as though it might have been an accident. Such enforced changes would doubtless give us a much duller *Hedda Gabler*, but Hollywood is notorious for its pragmatic interest in how the concluding scenes fit with what has gone before. Most important of all is the triumph of morality.

The second problem the film adaptation encounters is a more difficult one to solve, and relates to the way Ibsen writes dialogue. Even though the conversational form in the modern Ibsen play to a great extent resembles the way in which we actually talk, with everyday turns of phrase, scripted pauses, interrupted sentences and fumbling for certain words – traits which are also the basis of dialogue written for film – the dialogue is, all the same, created for the dramatic needs of the stage, where the way of building up dramatic situations differs from that of film. In Ibsen, it is the dialogue that keeps the action moving, a dramatic technique that he perfected. The filmatic ideal, on the other hand, is that dialogue follows the action. This is due to certain physical constraints that affect the stage but not film. What makes Ibsen's dialogue particularly demanding in a filmatic environment is that everything that is said is loaded with meaning, sometimes with double-meaning, and that the most important lines usually come shortly before the curtain falls. Granted, this applies more to a play like *Ghosts* than to *Hedda Gabler*, but consider all the same the long, densely packed dialogue between Hedda and Løvborg in the second act. You have to follow very closely indeed to pick up all the shifts and nuances. This is hard enough in the theatre, where the audience's attention is nonetheless exposed to fewer distractions. In a filmatic context, the audience will more rapidly lose patience. Movement is expected, either in the picture itself or by the camera moving and the eye will wander across the screen in search of something new to fasten attention on. So in a filmed adaptation there is a need to rewrite the dialogue so that it serves the action and not the other way round.

Yet the greatest difficulty in filming Ibsen's dramas with contemporary settings lies in the dramatic form of these plays, a difficulty that the historical plays do not suffer from. The action of *Hedda Gabler* takes place – as in so many other of Ibsen's dramas – indoors, in a sitting room and an adjacent back room. Over many years, Ibsen developed a dramatic form adapted to the needs of the static space of the theatre. In plays like *Hedda Gabler* and *A Doll's House* it is precisely the closed room that reinforces the feeling that both Nora and Hedda have limited freedom of movement and are cut off from the society surrounding them. In a film context, this limitation of space is a challenge, because film's distinctive quality is that it can present action from a number of places which can be spliced together in a natural flow in the editing process. Now of course there are examples of films in which the action takes place almost entirely indoors, and in the same house. But in such films the camera is often used to move around inside the room, often through several rooms, dwelling on detail and defining various zones as mysterious, or dangerous or private. In *A Doll's House* the letterbox, Helmer's office, and the living room would be used to underscore the prevailing dramatic mood, depending on where the action was taking place. In *Hedda Gabler,* the backroom with its portrait of General Gabler has a symbolic value, but the interior is otherwise little used to accentuate the dramatic tension. Tesman's library, for example, is wholly without interest for Hedda and for the audience, his historical writings on the subject of the folk arts of Brabant concern no-one but Tesman himself. For the most part, we stay in the salon, which is Hedda's domain. And in a filmatic context this poses the challenge of how to avoid a camera that is not too static, but on the contrary creates movement and drama in the visual composition.

In a theatre setting, the stage and the wings represent the physical dimension. When a character exits by a side-door and leaves the stage, he or she moves into an imaginary room. The static nature of the stage-space leads the audience to accept that we cannot follow to see what is on the other side of the door, unless of course there is a change of scene. This we accept as a being part of the nature of the theatrical experience. We do not, however, accept the same limitation in the world of film. Often we expect the camera to move along with the character, so that we become party to what happens beyond the door. In *Hedda Gabler* this is of critical importance for any planned adaptation of the play for the screen. Unlike *A Doll's House* or *Ghosts*, where the most important events take place on the stage, in the drawing room of the house, most of the dramatic events in *Hedda Gabler* take place offstage, and outside the house. We learn what happens out there via various reports that are related to Hedda. In film this would be an unsatisfactory solution, for the cinema audience demands to be where the action is. One possible way of dealing with this would be to insert a montage between the Second and Third Acts in which we see Løvborg knocking back the punch while he reads to Tesman at Brack's house and then them all going their separate ways thereafter to continue their partying elsewhere. And when Tesman comes home in the morning and tells Hedda what he did afterwards, this can be shown in a flashback in which we see Løvborg staggering along in the gutter and losing the manuscript, which Tesman finds.

But can what Brack relates concerning Løvborg in the Fourth Act be given visual representation in the same way? What really did happen to Løvborg between the Third and Fourth Acts, after he left Hedda for the last time? We know that at one point he went to Diana's boudoir, that they quarrelled, and that the gun went off. But we don't know the surrounding detail (Brack: "He was trying to take the pistol out of his pocket in order to threaten her? And it went off then? Or did she grab the gun from his hand, shoot him and put the pistol back in his pocket?"). Nor do we know whether Løvborg did anything before this. Here the film-maker has some choices to make. And as a cinema audience, it is Løvborg we want to follow and expect to follow, when he goes out into the streets with a pistol in his pocket, to see what happens next. This is where the action of the drama is. Aunt Rina's death is of less interest to us. If we have to wait for Brack before finally finding out what happened we are liable to feel cheated. But if we have already seen what happens, then Brack's later telling of the story to Hedda will be of little interest to us – this in spite of the fact that the scene is one of the dramatic peaks in the stage-play.

Let's say that in order to solve these problems the film has to get rid of the first scenes of the Fourth Act and go straight to Brack making his entrance and describing what happened to Løvborg, and that this is visually illustrated as he talks. Even so, the scene between Brack and Hedda will lose something here, because in Ibsen the greatest dramatic interest lies in hearing about these events, not in seeing them. To be more specific, in observing Hedda as she finds out how mistaken her assumptions were. This is not achieved if Brack's description is visually illustrated and the effect falls flat if we have already seen what happened.

So it really doesn't help very much when Jerry Wald gets Lauren Bacall to play Diana and gives her a few seductive songs to sing, nor that he asks Curtiz, Schulberg and Alton to add in these extra scenes, along with the rest of the changes. At the next screening Hedda seems both more wicked and less deep. At the test screening for the general public the audience gives the film the thumbs down, they couldn't see the point of portraying a woman like that. So the film never made it to the cinemas. MGM's 1953 Shakespeare film, *Julius Cæsar*, on the other hand, enjoyed great success, winning one Oscar and being nominated in four categories.

Why is it that Shakespeare succeeds in Hollywood and Ibsen does not, in spite of the fact that many of the film adaptations retain the dialogue in blank verse? First and foremost it is because Shakespeare's dramatic form is much closer to the narrative art of film than Ibsen's plays are. In Shakespeare, the action switches between several locations at the same time. His plays are full of action, battle scenes and murder, as well as young love. Add to this that Shakespeare's plays combine high and low culture, appealing to the ruffians standing at the back of the crowd as well as the courtiers in the boxes. Film as a medium does precisely the same thing, moving constantly between entertainment and profundity.

Shakespeare has, moreover, had enthusiastic ambassadors like Orson Welles, Franco Zeffirelli and Kenneth Branagh, something that Ibsen has thus far lacked, at least in Hollywood. But in the 1970s, two American films based on Ibsen's plays were made. One was *A Doll's House* (1973), directed by Joseph Losey, with Jane Fonda as Nora, the other *An Enemy of the People*, directed by George Schaefer and starring Steve McQueen as Dr Stockman. But despite the star casting, both productions are well outside the Hollywood system and regarded as peripheral films. On the other hand, it has been claimed that Steven Spielberg's *Jaws* is based on *An Enemy of the People*, not that Ibsen is credited with the storyline. There are also good grounds for claiming that Robert Benton's *Kramer vs Kramer* (1979), with Dustin Hoffman and Meryl Streep, is a continuation of *A Doll's House*, seen from Helmer's point of view. This indicates that Ibsen is a source of inspiration among certain Hollywood film-makers and that it is possible to be successful using his themes. So even though Ibsen's plays don't lend themselves as well as Shakespeare's to film adaptations that stick fairly closely to the text, it is still quite possible that Ibsen would have been in demand in Hollywood had he lived today.

Bibliography:

Asbjørn Aarseth: "Drama in the Narrow Room." In: *Ibsen on Screen*, edited by Jan Erik Holst and Astrid Sæther, Oslo 2000.
André Bazin: "Theater and Cinema." In: *What is Cinema?* Berkeley, 1967

Allardyce Nicoll: "Film Reality: The Cinema and the Theater." In: *Film and Theater*, edited by James Hurt, New Jersey, 1974.

Peter Craig Raimond. "Can Ibsen be Filmed?" In: *The Norseman*, Jan–Feb, 1952.

Helge Rønning: "From Snorre To Dante's Peak." In: *Ibsen on Screen*.

Raymond Williams: *Drama From Ibsen to Eliot*. London, 1952.

– – –

Audun Engelstad is currently a research scholar at the Institute for Media and Communication at the University of Oslo. His background is in literary studies but at the moment his research interests are concentrated on film, TV series, dramaturgy and popular culture. Some years ago he lectured on *A Doll's House* and *Hedda Gabler* to students at the Oslo Summer School.

AFTERWORD TO *THE MASTERBUILDER*

by Mari Lending

Put a pair of brackets around Hilde Wangel. With just two key strokes the whole metaphorical apparatus produced by the young lady is put in check, everything that makes *The Masterbuilder*, after a hundred years of psychoanalysis, a perfect example of Marcel Proust's literary horror: that a piece of work embodying a theory is like a gift without the price tag removed. With Hilde Wangel at the centre of the drama, Ibsen's play comes ready-interpreted. But when Hilde Wangel is put out of commission, the masterbuilder becomes something more than a broken-down old fool who is driven to his death by a wish to impress his demanding admirer. The play's many spires and towers can be rescued from a phallic, comprehensively eroticised, symbolic swamp. The play's banal psycho-fairytale discourse ('the troll in me', 'the bird of prey in you', 'the kingdom of Orangina') evaporates. In place of the stale old theme of the ageing man who fears youth generally, we see that *The Masterbuilder* is a technological-existential drama. Ibsen, the poet of modern times, describes the confrontation between two professions: builder and architect.

Hilde Wangle must nevertheless be allowed to pose two questions which lead directly to the professional and existential drama that her presence otherwise does its best to obscure. "Why don't you call yourself an 'architect', like the others?" she asks in the Second Act. "I'm not educated enough for that. What I know is mainly what I have taught myself," answers the masterbuilder. On another occasion, the talk is of books. Hilde Wangel is impressed by Solness' large collection and asks if he reads much. "I used to, before," replies the masterbuilder, and when Hilde assures him that she doesn't read books either – "not on your life" as she puts it, "I can't make any sense of it anyway" – Solness agrees: "That's exactly how I feel too."

The Masterbuilder is a drama of contemporary life. If one takes the play literally, in the sense that it is about a masterbuilder in a particular place, at a particular time, that is to say, provincial Norway in the 1890s, then one quickly sees the outlines of a drama of professional life. In other words: one need not look any further than the play's first stage directions, or in fact, before that, at the list of characters, to get a sense of what kind of drama is about to unfold: a drama of fate, based on the conflict between masterbuilder and architect. It is generally recognised that the opening scenes of Ibsen's dramas are of great significance: here the most important lines of conflict and themes are all hinted at. Ibsen students have, however, to be prepared to make an exception in the case of *The Masterbuilder*, as the first scene of the First Act opens with apparent trivialities in a country architect's office and some time passes before the plot's erotic magnet, Hilde Wangel, makes her entry. The precise description of the 'drawing office', however, along with the play's most brutal sentence – the character-listing of Knut Brovik as 'former architect, now assistant to Solness'– points directly to the play's tragic conclusion. The ending of *The Masterbuilder* is tragic not only because the play's main character dies, but also because it conforms so perfectly with the special tragic logic of Greek drama, which depends on the turning point at which jubilation turns to horror, when the show-off's pride is dashed to the ground and the hero recognises or understands something of fatal significance – with violent and often fateful consequences.

Solness embraces his own death willingly because it dawns on him that what he has created is worthless: "Look, there's the whole reckoning, all the way back as far as I can see. Nothing built, not really. And nothing sacrificed in order to build something either. Nothing, nothing – all of it," says Solness, before he climbs up and falls to his death.

In the most celebrated peripetia of world literature, this shattering revelation takes place in a single instant: when the distraught Oedipus realises that he has killed his father and lain with his mother. In Solness' case, the fateful and deadly insight comes in two parts and has been prepared for over a number of years. The first part is signalled by Solness challenging God; the related scene which describes how, ten years earlier, he addressed God while laying the wreath around the church spire in Lysanger. The masterbuilder shouts to the skies that he will no longer design churches, henceforth he will dedicate his life to building 'homes for people'. Solness speaks to God as though they were equals. Anyone can see how great the fall will be for someone of such pretensions and Solness talks about himself in a way that clearly alludes to the idea of the superman: 'Don't you agree with me, Hilde, that there are a few chosen people who have been given the power and the grace and the ability to *wish* for something, *desire* something, *will* something – so intensely – so mercilessly – that in the end they must get it. Don't you feel that?'

In the old masterbuilder we have an image of the architect as god-like, an idea that goes back to Plato's *Timaeus*. Here the demiurge creates the universe, but not out of nothing like the Christian god. The demiurge transforms already existing material into stars, planets, gods and people according to certain ideal forms – sense is instilled in the soul and the soul in the body. The Timaeus dialogue is both architectonic, nature-philosophical and mythological. The world is a construction that is held together by specific architectonic principles: the creation of the universe is described in terms of mathematics, geometry, proportion, regularity and models of calculation, such as space, lines, proportionality and depth. It is the demiurge, he who can create order out of chaos and erect, structure and shape the universe from top to bottom, who lurks behind the idea of the omnipotent architect. The figure has its origins in Antiquity and has lived through the Renaissance, survived Modernism, until the death of the architect in the 1960s became a theoretical reality on a par with the death of the author. What this means is that this idea of the omnipotent demiurge has hibernated within popular culture, where it regularly appears in the shape of the ever-mythical role of architect. "Have you seen the new addition to the Guggenheim?" *Seinfeld's* George answers when he meets the It-girl from high school days again after twenty years, and she contemptuously asks what he has done with his life? The role of architect endows George with heroism and romance, with an additional dimension of power and glory, art and science, beauty and truth.

Halvard Solness creates not just a cautious association with the traditional role of the architect when he, in stating that he will henceforth build homes and not churches, turns from the collective to the private; with his repeated and exalted assurances that he will build *homes for people,* the masterbuilder also conjures up an affinity with God, in his ambition to create not just places to live, but also life and happiness.

The second element in the insight that leads Solness to his death touches less on the cultural aspects of the architect's role and rather more on the historical and pragmatic realities associated with the role. Despite the insistence – from the title onwards – that Halvard Solness is a masterbuilder and not an architect, he runs a successful architectural firm. Whereas most Norwegian architectural firms in the 1890s consisted of the architect himself, possibly with an assistant and a wife who kept the books, this is a fairly large office, with three employees: the trained architect, Knut Brovik, his son the draughtsman, Ragnar Brovik, and the bookkeeper, Kaja Fosli. It emerges that Ragnar Brovik is in his early thirties. If we give his father an existence outside the realm of fiction, then we can assume that the elder Brovik is around seventy years old and probably trained at the technical college in Hanover, or possibly Berlin, in the 1850s. In a Norwegian context that makes him one of only a handful of professionally trained architects. According to one not entirely reliable source, there were nine architects in Oslo – of whom the oldest was Ch. H Grosch, who died in 1865. A nationwide registration in 1902 reveals that there were eighty-five architects in Christiania, twelve in Bergen, thirteen in Trondheim and another eleven working in various towns, in other words, a grand total of 121 practising architects. One purpose of the registration was to establish judicial, economic and collegial guidelines for the architectural profession, not least in order to create a distinction between architects with a theoretical training and other professionals within the building trade, such as masterbuilders and contractors. The architect was to be the commissioning party's representative in meetings with those handling the practical side of the building work. It was his responsibility to ensure the best interests of the project and he should have no financial interest in the building process. The analphabetic autodidact Solness is the very type of the masterbuilder that the architectural profession wished to prevent from using the title 'architect'. Thanks to his wife's inheritance, he has established himself by dividing up land into building plots and designing, building and selling homes in the parklands surrounding her childhood home and is thereby financially involved in every aspect of the building project. Had he wished to, however, he was perfectly entitled to call himself 'architect' as 'architect' was not a protected professional title. Not until the Royal Decree of 25 April 1986 was the title 'civil architect' associated with defined criteria. In Solness' day, anyone could call himself an architect, as, for example, the mastermason, Harald Olsen, did in 1899 when he designed and built Christiania Glasmagasin.

That Solness does not adopt the more flashy 'architect' as his title is possibly explained by the fact that he does, after all, have a sense of common decency. As a young man he was employed in Knut Brovik's architectural firm. A financially advantageous marriage provided him with the opportunity to take over the practise himself and demote the architect to assistant. Brovik himself describes Solness' social mobility thus: "Started out as a poor boy from the country, – and stands here now as the leading man in your field." It is not, however, in the conflict between the upstart Solness and the degraded Brovik that the masterbuilder – architect drama is most clearly articulated. This particular conflict has been sidelined long before the play opens. Brovik's impotence is demonstrated for the last time when the masterbuilder heartlessly lets him die without granting him his only wish – specifically, Solness' signature on his son's drawings for a villa for a young married couple, and thereby, more generally, Solness' blessings on Ragnar's possible future career as an architect. The real drama of *The Masterbuilder* is the tension between the ageing builder and the aspiring young architect. It is the contrast between the universally dominating Solness and the cautious, taciturn Ragnar that is foreshadowed in the opening scene and that leads to the tragic logic of the play that drives Solness to his death.

The Masterbuilder begins as the firm's only architect is about to die and the young draughtsman is in the process of discovering his talent – as an architect. Even though Solness constantly tries to undermine the importance of the Broviks, it is obvious who is responsible for the technical side of the firm's activities: "Because I needed Ragnar myself. And the old man too. He's so good at working out bearing capacities and cubic content – and all that type of stuff, you know," the builder admits at one point to his friend, Dr Heldal. And through the young married couple's enthusiasm for Ragnar's design for their villa, a picture emerges of a modern housebuilder whose taste and personal preferences are given the architect's attentive ear – in contrast to the masterbuilder's mildly hysterical and decidedly authoritarian experience of drawing for a generalised category of 'people'. And if the masterbuilder's grinding condescension is an attempt to undermine Ragnar's talent, the young man's ability shines through the subtext with great and critical power and finds expression in a recognition that is abrupt, ambivalent and filled with anxiety: "But this Ragnar, – he can't, not at any price, be allowed to show what he can do"; "If he shows what he can do, then he'll knock me flat. Crush me – just the way I did with his father." This ends with a preliminary crescendo in the outburst: "He is the young man who stands ready to knock on my door. And make a definite end of Masterbuilder Solness and all his ways."

The reader is given only a few hints as to what type of villas the masterbuilder has been mass-producing. But one might guess that his success is based on the Swiss villa style, typically designed by masterbuilders of the time, that was so popular in the second half of the 19th century, richly adorned with Solness' beloved towers, spires and turrets. The text does provide one distinctly architectural clue and the remark, from the play's opening scene, also undermines the idea that the masterbuilder's fear of youth is a conventional conflict of generations. When old Brovik tries to persuade Solness to sign his son's drawings, he tells him that the young couple "liked very much the ideas he showed them. They thought it was something completely new, they said". Solness replies, as sarcastic as he is frightened: "Aha – new! None of that old-fashioned nonsense such as I used to build!" In this sequence, Ibsen places *The Masterbuilder* at the centre of the heated debate about historicism, as well as the equally emotive discussion on architecture as a profession and the training of architects that was a feature of Norwegian magazines and newspapers in the last decades of the 19th century. The old masterbuilder's homemade 'nonsense' is challenged by "something completely new" as represented by Ragnar Brovik's drawings, a nascent modernism that had begun to appear throughout Europe in the 1890s, not least in the form of villa architecture.

What *The Masterbuilder* illustrates is Henrik Ibsen's criticism of the dilettante. It is the old masterbuilder's gradual realisation of his own technical shortcomings, his inadequate insight into art and science, that drives him to his death. The tyrannical amateur, Halvard Solness, crumples when he is exposed to a genuine architectural talent in the shape of Ragnar Brovik. The discrepancy between the masterbuilder's superhuman fantasies and the actual work he leaves behind – buildings with no meaning, no depth, no imagination – is insupportable. Solness has too many character flaws to fall with the style and beauty of the classical tragic hero. The shattering insight, "Nothing, nothing – not any of it" is, all the same, perfectly tragic and human, and it is this which grants the masterbuilder his fall from a height which he has never previously been close to attaining.

– – –

Mari Lending was born in 1969. She has an M.A. in Literary Science (1997) and a PhD in the theory of architecture (2005). She has worked for some years as a critic of literature and architecture, has written essays and also edited a number of books.

ALWAYS RELEVANT, HA HA HA

Afterword to *John Gabriel Borkman* by Pernille Rygg

One of the first things I wrote was a parody of Ibsen. It was a good –
though stolen – idea and not very well executed, but it did, of course,
include the most important elements: the betrayed child, the travel-
ler who brings forgotten secrets back into play, masculine hubris, a
clear subtext and a touch of nature mysticism. Of course it's possible
to do an 'Instant Ibsen', a condensed version of his collected works, as
has been done with Shakespeare's plays. It is, after all, almost a truism
that the really distinctive authorial voices are those which most easily
lend themselves to parody.

"Can you imagine it, he went completely bankrupt," ran one of the
lines in my not-very-impressive parody. And everyone will naturally
recognise Ibsen. Just as naturally, there is another necessary ingredient: the element of social debate. Ibsen's trademark, his 'own brand'.

'Always relevant' we used to say in my family about Ibsen, and
laugh. That's to say, we younger ones laughed, because for the people
of my parents' and grandparents' generation there were no audibly
inverted commas around the words 'always relevant'. Ibsen *was* always relevant, provocative, sharp, controversial, in spite of the fact
that almost a complete century lay between him and us, in spite of the
statues and the canonisation, in spite of Hamsun, modernism, countless essays by countless schoolchildren and constant performances.

As it happens, I come from a family that, to use a word that sounds
almost as archaic as, for example, 'backfish' (teenage girl) or 'sigaret-
tetui' (cigarette case), could be described as 'teatergal' (theatre-mad).
Both my parents were actors in their younger years and my maternal

grandfather worked throughout his long life at the National Theatre. He had seen some of the theatrical greats like Eleonora Duse and Sarah Bernhard on stage (no, no-one knows anymore who they were, but in my family we were familiar with these names from about the age of ten) and he knew and worked with Bjørnstjerne Bjørnson's son when he was the director of the theatre, so in one sense he was an *almost* direct link to the literary era of the Great Four and to Ibsen himself. Always relevant.

It's obvious: when you've sat in the red plush seats at the National Theatre since the age of five, wearing your crepe stockings and your best dress to see Ibsen plays, the claim of 'always relevant' is liable to call forth ironic laughter by the time you've reached your teens. And a good job too, because this goes for everyone, not just theatre-mad families: just how provoked can you actually be by an author whom your *teacher* tells you is controversial? How sharp, controversial and super-relevant can the works of an author your *grandfather* admires really be?

Obviously, no author should be judged by the degree of snotty teenage laughter he rouses, or by his inability to raise the temperature in the classroom. But it is no accident that it is Ibsen who is humiliated in this way in Dag Solstad's novel, *Genanse og verdighet* (*Shyness and dignity*). It has partly to do with his iconic status and partly with the fact that one really has to dig deep in Ibsen to find the unfamiliar nuances, since even the subtexts have established themselves so solidly among the set texts for schools and universities ("Thank you for the light"). In Solstad's novel, the teacher Rukla is ecstatic when he finds a 'trembling' in one of the stage directions for a line in *The Wild Duck* (Dr Relling: [with a trembling in his voice]) and 'trembling' is a new discovery, a nuance, a mystery. A mystery? In Ibsen? Is that possible?

Perhaps it is, even if it means having to study the stage directions. But more than most other authors of classic status, Ibsen is a victim of the solid and persistent demand that he be 'always relevant'. Relevant for today. Incisive. It is as though his status as a classic isn't enough somehow. Poor Ibsen is condemned, throughout eternity's eternities, to present problems for debate. It is not the nicest of fates, something like being condemned in perpetuity to rage furiously from a soapbox in hell's own Speakers' Corner.

This applies to *John Gabriel Borkman* as well as to the other plays. Perhaps to an even greater extent to *John Gabriel Borkman*, because in the educated public's assessment of the Maestro Ibsen – the kind of comment overheard during the interval at the theatre – *Borkman* is usually counted among the weaker works. The old man has one masterpiece left to write, *When We Dead Awaken*, and *Borkman* is, if not exactly a rest, then a work weak enough to make the construction and the method a little too visible. Not quite up to standard, then, but a very proficient piece of work nonetheless.

The ironic, sneering teenager that I once was could get very worked up by these interval comments ("He was good, wasn't he?" "It got better during the Second Act"); if they really meant anything, these plays, these artistic experiences, then shouldn't they do a bit more than turn us all into amateur theatre critics? Shouldn't they mean something? Change us in some way? No doubt it was the trembling I was looking for, without knowing it.

As a result I stopped going to the theatre as often. Young Erhardt Borkman travels abroad to get away from the generation above him – though it isn't easy to believe in any liberated future for the play's young characters, in spite of the consummate bashing the old ones get in *John Gabriel Borkman*. Things really don't look all that promising for Erhardt.

Well then, where is it, the 'always relevant' element of this play that perhaps doesn't quite make it to the top of the collected works? Where is the trembling, the resonance? Is it in the parallel between Ibsen's and Borkman's rampant capitalism, and our own? Parallels that at the moment only seem to increase rather than decrease? Borkman as Enron boss, for example, as the man behind it all when the entire Argentinean nation went completely bankrupt two years ago?

Or is it in the more spiritual side, in Ibsen's biography: the dreams of greatness and the frightening, eerie results of bringing to life things that lie buried, the Faustian, the ur-modern. If you dig up what is buried, be it industrial metals or the secrets of the soul, are unknown forces released, which are as likely to be as destructive as they are creative?

Or is it the old man's tormented, uneasy and ambivalent support for youth that casts a harsh light on an age when youth has become dogma and rebels turn into saleable items of pop culture within the space of a few seconds?

You have to look for your own trembling, find your own reso-nance. And mine, what moves me most when I read Borkman, is actually nothing like this, but something almost prosaic. A strange hope, you might call it, a contrary and somewhat frightening faith. And this is how it goes, in an everyday version formulated by a friend with a great and dogged sense of justice: cheats never prosper.

She'll say this on any number of different occasions. When some high-flying financier crashes to the ground, or an over-praised mar-riage breaks up. It was on the cards. You can't lie and cheat and bodge and fudge, neither socially nor spiritually, and get away with it. One way or another, you will get your come-uppance. In the form of spiritual anguish. Or some physical illness. Ruin, in one form or another.

Cheats never prosper. Anything else would be almost intolerable. It is the thought that cheats never prosper that leads us to assume – or hope – that rich people are unhappy, that creeps have marital troubles, that bad neighbours are hated by their children. Even if they get away with it on a purely social level, there is something that works to ensure that, sooner or later, in their souls, in their fates, they will have to pay.

That cheats never prosper, that one gets one's just deserts in the end, is of course a widely-held belief and an age-old hope. It is almost certainly the origin of great constructions like religions, like heaven and hell, for if justice should not properly triumph in a social sense here in life, then at least there was the hope that it would be handed down afterwards. My friend is of course not religious, but her notion that cheats never prosper here in life is also a metaphysical one.

For it is, after all, a faith? It might very well not be the case. The slipperiest of financial wheelers and dealers may have a happy life, the bad man be loved by his children and the greatest manipulator may enjoy peace of mind. Maybe. It is a dreadful possibility and a big chance to take and risky games are thrilling, for players and specta-tors alike. It is a game of chance we follow in the tabloids' revelations about famous people of our own times, with as much hunger for transgression and prosperity, as for a fall. For those of us looking on, the fall is often experienced as a relief. Ha! He took a tumble there, that high-flyer. See, that rock star ended up a junkie. Transgression, at the very least, costs.

For an Ibsen, as for anyone today who has abandoned the notion of a literal heaven and hell, there remain two arenas in which cheats can be exposed and judgement handed down – the social and the spiritual. Despite the tabloids, the social often fails to deliver. But the spiritual, fate – does that fail to deliver too?

Before Ibsen lets Borkman die, he must acknowledge, he must realise his error. That is the whole point, the unavoidable inevitability. Maybe forgiveness comes then, maybe he can just let go, whatever – there can be no end before this happens, before the cheating, the betrayal of love, has revealed itself and been seen. Psychologists and spiritual therapists will all applaud

And the need for this, the longing within an old man to create a space where the miracle of acknowledgement can take place – on paper, that is, within the theatre, now that the church is no longer able to provide such rituals and life cannot guarantee them – that need, that longing, that faith, that hope and that comfort, there is a trembling in that, a resonance.

Always relevant, you might say.

– – –

Pernille Rygg was born in 1963 in Oslo. Her first novel was *Sommerfuglefekten* (The Butterfly Effect), published in 1995. She studied history and ethnology at the University of Oslo, and has worked as a set painter on film and tv. Her first book was entered for Gyldendal's competition for crime novels, and it has been translated into nine languages, including English, French, Italian and German. A second crime novel, *Det gyldne snitt* (The Golden Section), followed in 2000. Her novel *Hundehjertet* (Dog Heart) was published in 1998.

THE DREAM OF SOMETHING MORE

Afterword to *When We Dead Awaken*
by Erling Sandmo

What is *When We Dead Awaken* really about? There is no easy answer to the question and many have tried. Some have tried to explain
the play in terms of its subtitle, "A dramatic epilogue". The subtitle
can be interpreted in two ways that both seem to offer a strong and
direct meaning: *When We Dead Awaken* can be read as an epilogue
both to Ibsen's long array of plays and to his long life as a writer – as
a bitter look back on both his work and his life. But it is by no means
certain that this is the case.

Merely an Epilogue?

Ibsen's oeuvre opens with *Catilina* and with the often quoted and
sometimes gently ridiculed lines

> I must! I must; a voice commands
> From the soul's depths, – I will obey.
> I have the power and courage for something
> More, something greater than this life.

Here we find in fact the main themes of *When We Dead Awaken:* the
calling, ambition, being true to one's self and the dream of exceeding
the limits of one's own earthly life. In *When We Dead Awaken* this
dream of something higher is transformed to a concrete, physical act
on the stage, with Rubek and Irene wandering up on the mountain.
Here they get caught in a landslide: part of the glacier breaks off and

'spins downwards at a furious pace'; Rubek and Irene are wiped out, becoming indistinct at first and then vanishing completely in all the white, as though they were letters on the page being rubbed out.

Read as an epilogue to his oeuvre, this is a brutal and pessimistic conclusion. The ambition to attain great heights ends in death, in the grave, in disappearance – and perhaps even in oblivion, if we consider the play's last breath, the distant sound of Maja's enduring song from the depths far below. Read as Ibsen's final thoughts on his own life, *When We Dead Awaken* is equally bleak. Rubek is the Artist, the man who put art and the idea of 'the calling' before life, thereby condemning both himself and those closest to him to an existence of emptiness and sterility. It is tempting to strike a parallel with Ibsen himself. He is recalled as being small, old, anxious and vain. He was the greatest dramatist of his age; but when, from his regular seat at the Grand, he looks back over his phenomenal career, when he writes his own epilogue, it is Rubek he sees: Rubek, who preferred art to life and ended out in the cold, the abyss, death.

When someone comes

When We Dead Awaken can be read like this. But such a reading is too simple. *When We Dead Awaken* is a much more complex play than this interpretation allows. It is therefore impossible to draw simple parallels with Ibsen's own life – in the sense that such parallels cast nothing more than a superficial light on the play. Biographical interpretations of great literature rarely teach us much about the most interesting aspect of it: its very greatness. And *When We Dead Awaken* is undoubtedly great drama, in more than one sense

Is it, for example, true that Rubeks's tragedy is that he has put art before life? Hardly. The play opens with the laidback, resigned conversation between himself and Maja outside the spa hotel, and Maja is essentially Rubek's attempt to choose 'life' – however one interprets that. He has made her a lot of promises he has failed to keep; he promised to take her with him up to the heights and show her 'all the glories of the world', but none of it has happened and they are both disappointed. At the beginning of the Second Act they continue the conversation and are in melancholy agreement that the relationship between them has hardly been more than a way of passing the time.

And love as a way of passing the time is intolerable: best they go their separate ways.

In the first of these conversations they talk about the train journey up through Norway, and it crystallises into a beautiful metaphor of a life that passes by without ever actually having anything to do with the living:

Professor Rubek. (…) Now we were really home. Because the train stopped at all the small stations, even though nothing was happening.

Fru Maja. Why did it stop so completely, when there was nothing happening?

Professor Rubek. Don't know. No one got off, no one boarded. Yet the train remained stationary for an eternity. And at every station I could hear two linesmen walking along the station, one had a lamp in his hand. And they were talking, muted and empty in the night.

Fru Maja. Yes, you're right there. There are always two men walking along and talking–

Professor Rubek. – and saying nothing.

The poverty of life weighs heavily on Rubek. "That is what explains the flat and lifeless dialogue between Maja and Rubek at the beginning of the First Act," writes Atle Kittang. But isn't that dialogue both concentrated and living? The language here is so dense, so precise – and when Rubek and Maja discuss the journey, they together develop the metaphorical aspect of it. In the lines quoted above, it is Maja who points out the universality of Rubek's little story about the night on the train, and he who at once follows up her observation.

This is the way people who know and like each other well speak to each other, as Rubek and Maja like each other, in their melancholy way. When such dialogue seems flat and lifeless on the stage, it is perhaps because it is undramatic in a way that only really intimate conversations are. And it is by no means certain that the only topic of conversation is Rubek's acknowledgement of the poverty of life; it may well be that it is also about their common recognition of the quiet evanescence of life and of their own lack of closeness. The marriage, the house and villa by the Taunitz, all the worldly wealth and the 'respectable social circle' cannot disguise the experience of existence as a slow search for nothing.

We are presented with a very modern attitude towards life. It recalls Albert Camus' view of life as essentially absurd. And even though the opening of *Catilina* seems to presage themes in Ibsen's epilogue, it seems strangely old-fashioned after reading *When We Dead Awaken*, like remote history. It is remarkable that the two plays are the work of the same dramatist. It is easier to see the connection between *When We Dead Awaken* and later modernist works. "A Game of Chess", one of the poems in T.S. Eliot's *The Wasteland*, contains a dialogue between a woman who longs to live and a husband who sees only death wherever he looks. There are also strong resemblances between *When We Dead Awaken* and Samuel Beckett's *Waiting for Godot*, with its two tramps waiting for someone to come who will make something happen, but who never arrives.

In *When We Dead Awaken*, however, someone does indeed come: Irene and Ulfheim. They personify Art and Life in a much more direct sense than Rubek and Maja and they divide them: Rubek follows Irene and Maja follows Ulfheim. Both have or acquire a faith that something will be revealed to them. Maja is disappointed. Ulfheim turns out not to be the magnificent predator he at first sight appeared to be and in his company Maja becomes a stilted parody of the self that emerges in the conversations she has with Rubek.

Not so with Irene. She has depth and she has power – the power to release Rubek from the shabbiness of life, to take him up with her towards the heights he has always dreamt of attaining. The ascent then ends in the fall to their deaths. But from the very start it has been clear that Irene cannot give Rubek what he dreams of getting from her: the redemption of art as a way of life. And yet once she too lived for such a redemption. She dreamt that she who had once been Rubek's model, a participant in the creative process, would be able to take part in the great crossing, the crossing of the divide between art and life, between eternity and sensuality. Instead Rubek betrayed both her and art. It cost her her soul, as she expresses it at the end of the First Act, staring rigidly at him: "I gave you my young, living soul. I stood there, empty inside – soulless. *That* was what I died of, Arnold."

By her own account, in the days since this betrayal, Irene has lived an empty and destructive life, despite the fact that it appears to have been rich in incident by comparison with Rubek's. She has been one of the living dead. And she persuades him that he too has been dead since they created that great work of art together, the sculpture 'Resurrection Day'. But their last, absurd search for life ends, of course, in the finality of death.

Rubek does not see what many of Ibsen's commentators have pointed out: that Irene is mad. Her behaviour is evidence of great and dangerous confusion and the fact that her chaperone, the nurse, travels with a suitcase containing a straitjacket makes it quite clear that in the universe of the play, Irene *is* insane.

Art's hold on life

But Irene will not relinquish her dream of transcendence and she gives it back to Rubek at a time when he seems to have given up and come to terms with an absurd and modern existence. With that, her madness becomes of secondary importance. The dream is not in itself insanity, but an underlying theme in all of Ibsen's writing and the basis of what Atle Kittang has called Ibsen's 'heroism', the existential desire to find better and more exalted ways of living than merely being content to be oneself.

In *When We Dead Awaken*, this desire is the desire for a fusion between art and life, and of a presence in something other and more than the lowly and the workaday. Rubek and Irene follow the dream and die; Maja and Ulfheim live on, dreamlessly. Thus the play can be interpreted as an account of the impossibility of transcendence. But one of the fascinations of the play is that it demonstrates, at the same time, the very opposite. Beyond the horizon of the characters in the play, the drama is overtaken by the work of art that is its prehistory, 'Resurrection Day'.

Originally, 'Resurrection Day' was a statue of Irene as the young, lone, pure, resurrected woman. Rubek's 'betrayal' of her and of art lies in the fact that he relocated her statue to a larger sculptural group without even allocating it a central place. 'Let us at the most call it a middle-ground figure – or some such', as Rubek says towards the close of the Second Act, to Irene's distress. In its final form the sculpture now shows a base with cracks in the earth out of which humans with bestial faces swarm. In the foreground a man sits with his feet held fast in the crust of the earth. He is trying to wash his hands clean: Rubek calls him 'regret for a life forfeited'.

While he relates all this, Rubek sits on a stone at the front of the stage, by a stream. He knots his fingers in anguish. At first Irene stands on the other side of the stream, leaning against a rock wall; later she sits down, a little closer. Vigdis Ystad is one of several commentators who have pointed out that the scenic imagery in the Second Act of *When We Dead Awaken* gradually fuses with the final version of 'Resurrection Day'. By contrast, the Third Act recreates the original version of the work of art, the only difference being that the artist himself has become a part of it.

This aspect of the play is a central part of its strong atmosphere of desolation, its dense aura of inevitability. The dream of crossing the boundary between life and art is in vain, for the boundary itself is an illusion. The characters on the stage are incapable of acknowledging that they are not free, that they are travelling through a landscape in which their fates have already been carved in stone.

The end of *When We Dead Awaken*, with the death of Rubek and Irene in the avalanche and the final line, the nurse's 'Pax vobiscum!', is strikingly similar to the concluding avalanche scene in *Brand*, where the last thing heard is a voice that cries – in Latin – 'through the thunderous rumbling': "He is the god of love". Rubek and Irene are thereby not only captured in 'Resurrection Day' – *When We Dead Awaken* becomes an epilogue to the whole of Ibsen's long line of plays in the sense that it repeats an earlier, fatal event.

This fate-laden fusion of life and art also turns *When We Dead Awaken* into a highly abstract drama. The landscape in which the characters move is higher with each passing act and is thus also a landscape of thought, a metaphor for something big, something existential and perhaps also something metaphysical. Precisely *what* that might be is not easy to say. Maybe *When We Dead Awaken* is about the desire for an almost abstract transcendence, a transcendence of pure form, so to speak, the certainty that it must be possible to search for something other and more than this dusty, protracted life down here. Rubek knows – or must believe – that there is something more than a life that denies art and a meaningless everyday life. The thought that there must be something more is much stronger than any precise notion of what the 'more' and the 'higher' might actually be.

The landscape of transcendence

Ibsen himself thought that his plays had to be considered in context. For this reason a lot of the literature about Ibsen is concerned with comparing them to see what light they shed on each other. *When We Dead Awaken* is rich in references to Ibsen's other plays. But it also points outwards, out of the oeuvre, towards ideas with a general contemporary currency and the artistic preoccupations of the time.

Rubek and Irene struggle towards the peaks of existence and head for the mountaintop, to a place that is 'people-free, purified of people', as Ulfheim puts it, halfway through the First Act. This break with the claustrophobic, limiting society of humans and the journey out into desolate and dangerous nature is a recurring theme of contemporary art and literature. The journey towards the cold heights becomes an image of the search for great understanding. The clearest example of this is the philosopher Friedrich Nietzsche, who is often regarded as an intellectual relative of Ibsen. His major works, *Thus Spake Zarathustra* (1883–85) and *Towards a Genealogy of Morals* (1887), both make connections between transition and freedom – and movement out into unknown and unpredictable nature. *Towards a Genealogy of Morals* has become notorious for its motto about 'setting the blond beast free', but Nietzsche's use of the bird of prey as a metaphor for the transcendental person, the superman, is in full parallel with Maja's description of the crushed Rubek as a 'tame bird of prey'. And towards the end of the play Ulfheim catches sight of Rubek and Irene on their way up towards the peak. Then he calls Rubek only 'bird of prey', the tame has been freed.

There is a famous painting by the German artist, Caspar David Friedrich (1774–1840), entitled 'The Wanderer over the Misty Sea'. It depicts a black-clad man with a stick who is standing alone on a mountaintop and looking down at the clouds. His back is turned to the viewer. The painting is often used in contexts where Nietzsche's writings are illustrated and it is very tempting to regard it as a portrait of Nietzsche himself – partly because the man seems to have a certain similarity to the philosopher, but first and foremost because it illustrates a physical and spiritual transcending of the limits of the human. Seen in this light it is also a striking visualisation of Rubek's dream of reaching the heights, where all the glories of the world will reveal themselves.

Historically speaking, this is of course quite wrong: the painting is from 1818, long before both Ibsen and Nietzsche's time. It seems probable that they both saw this famous work of art and derived inspiration from it. But there is a cultural chasm between early and late 19th century dreams of conquering heights. Friedrich was a Christian nature-romantic. Nietzsche's and Ibsen's visions of transcendence sprang from a quite different and modern frustration at the barriers erected by bourgeois society.

And the use of heights and the purity of the cold crops up again and again in much of the most futuristic art of the late 19th century – not least in the world of music. The composer, Richard Strauss (1864–1949), was intensely preoccupied with Nietzsche and set *Thus Spake Zarathustra* to music in 1896, three years before Ibsen wrote *When We Dead Awaken*. Strauss would later also write a symphonic poem based on Nietzsche's *Antichrist*, but held back from the controversies of the text and its title. The result was *An Alpine Symphony* (1915). Here Nietzsche's philosophy is transformed into a concrete and detailed description of the ascent of a mountain, with the wanderers setting out in the half-light of dawn, reaching the top in the blinding light of freedom and understanding, and descending once more to the lowly and the obscure – existentially transformed. The parallel with *When We Dead Awaken* is striking.

An older but perhaps even more significant composer in the context of our discussion is Richard Wagner (1813–1883). His great operas are also about the pull of redemption and acknowledgement. *When We Dead Awaken* does in fact contain a direct reference to Wagner, in that loaded scene towards the end of the Second Act where Rubek and Irene sit throwing rose petals into the stream and recalling the time they spent together by the Taunitz. On that occasion too they played by the water.

Professor Rubek. And you had the birds swimming in the stream. They were water lilies, which you –

Irene. They were white swans.

Professor Rubek. Yes, swans is what I meant. And I recall I fastened a large, shaggy leaf to one of the swans. I do believe it was a dock leaf –

Irene. And that turned it into Lohengrin's boat, with the swan drawing it.

Wagner's *Lohengrin* (1850) is about a hero who is duty-bound to search for the Holy Grail, the very incarnation of the Mystery. This obligation compels him to forsake all else, all earthly life. The journey is made in a ship drawn by a swan – which Irene identifies herself with in the dialogue above: it is she who carries Rubek onward in his search.

Lohengrin is just one of the Wagner operas that circle round the relationship between loneliness, renunciation and the journey towards a desolate goal where realisation is attained – round the idea of death as the final release. Both *Tristan and Isolde* (1865) and *Parsifal* (1882) share this basic motif with *When We Dead Awaken*, and the similarities illuminate the sense in which *When We Dead Awaken* is a metaphysical mystery play rather than a piece of bourgeois realism. It is interesting to see how two of the most famous foreign commentators on the play both note the connection between Wagner and Ibsen. James Joyce reviewed *When We Dead Awaken* in 1900 and remarked on the Lohengrin scene, and in his 1933 study 'Richard Wagner's suffering and greatness', Thomas Mann related Ibsen's epilogue to *Parsifal*, Wagner's last opera: 'I am used to looking upon them as one, feeling them as one, these two formal dramas of farewell, these last words before the eternal silence.'

Was Ibsen familiar with this music? The opportunities to experience opera – and in even higher degree symphonic music – were very much more limited in his day than they are now. Yet he was certainly familiar with Wagner: Wagner was one of the towering artistic figures of the 19th century, and Ibsen spent many years of his life in Germany. Strauss, on the other hand, was probably unknown to him. The point here, however, is not one of any direct influence, but rather that Ibsen's strange and self-referential epilogue is not just the writer's own judgement on himself, but a work in intense dialogue with its own times and the great search for something other and more. It was written while Mahler was at work on his early, great symphonies, in which the landscape of realisation is created by sound and is opened in time. Bruckner wrote his last, unfinished symphony and died in 1896. In an article on the composer's 'dark mystery', Erling Gulbrandsen wrote of how listening to Bruckner's symphonies is an experience that can lead to the transcendence of boundaries. There are two main components to the experience: the first is the sensation of fighting one's way upwards, in the face of opposition, to achieve a goal, a victory; the second is 'the celebration of a rousing love of life'. This occurs in music which is structured as a careful movement upwards towards ever higher levels, up towards a final tonal place where all opposition is resolved in shining harmony. In Bruckner we find a realisation of the transcendence that Rubek dies for, albeit in another art form. Each in his own way, each in his own place, the old men, Ibsen and Bruckner, reach out toward something other and more than this life down here.

So much has been said, and so much can be said, about *When We Dead Awaken*. But let this be the conclusion: the dramatic epilogue is packed with the same ideas and concepts that we find in Ibsen's artistic contemporaries who dreamt big dreams of something more. And Ibsen's final act as a dramatist is magnificent. While turning and looking back, he also embraces his own time: the epilogue is the harbinger of something new. Never before had Ibsen seen so far into the future as he did at the moment he lay down his pen.

Bibliography

Tom Eide, *Ibsens dialogkunst: Etikk og eksistens i Når vi døde vågner* (Oslo 2001) *Ibsen's dialogue: Ethics and Existence in When the Dead Awaken*

Erling E. Gulbrandsen & Øivind Varkøy (ed.), *Musikk og mysterium: Fjorten essay om grensesprengende musikalsk erfaring* (Oslo 2004) *Music and Mystery: fourteen essays on music experience that transcends boundaries*

Jørgen Dines Johansen, *Ind i natten: Seks kapitler om Ibsens sidste skuespil* (Odense 2004) *Into the Night: Six chapters on Ibsen's last play*

Atle Kittang, Ibsens heroisme: *Frå Brand til Når vi døde vågner* (Oslo 2002) *Ibsen's heroism: from* Brand *to* When We Dead Awaken

Lisbeth P. Wærp (ed.), *Livet på likstrå: Henrik Ibsens* Når vi døde vågner (Oslo 1999) (contains the texts referred to by Joyce, Mann and Ystad) *Life laid out: Henrik Ibsen's* When We Dead Awaken

– – –

Erling Sandmo was born in 1963. Historian. He is a music reviewer for NRK P2 radio and a columnist in *Dagbladet* and *Morgenbladet*. Sandmo's publications include *Mordernes forventninger: kriminalitetshistoriske essay* (The Murderers expectations: a criminality historical essay) 1998; *Voldssamfunnets undergang: om disiplineringen av Norge på 1600-tallet* (The decline of the violent society: on the disciplining of Norway in the 17th century) (1999) and *Siste ord: Høyesterett i norsk historie, 1905–1965* (Last words: the Supreme Court in Norwegian history 1905–1965) (2005). He is a researcher at the Institute for Social Research 1997–2005, and from 2006 senior lecturer in middle-period history at the University of Oslo.